THUNDER

STORIES FROM THE FIRST TOUR

To Jim Smith —
The warrior with
the pen!

Welcome Home!

D1091349

Jack Heslin

JACK HESLIN

outskirts
press

Outskirts Press, Inc.
http://www.outskirtspress.com

ISBN: 978-1-9772-0035-8

To my wife of over 50 years, Jean, and my four children — John, Joan, Jim, and Joe — who paid the price for my life of service and without whom there would be no "Jack" Heslin.

Table of Contents

Prologue

No one who hasn't thundered through the skies of Vietnam in a helicopter in combat can know what that experience was like. Most helicopter crews had more than one tour in Vietnam. Most had their aircraft hit by enemy fire many times. Many of us had been shot down at least once. We knew that combat flying in Vietnam was living on the edge all the time. Over the battlefields, you could hear the thunder of the rotor blades that put fear in the hearts of the enemy ... and brought comfort to our troops on the ground. The Vietnam War was a constant cacophony of manmade thunder.

Long ago, in a different galaxy — I remember. Then again, it was just yesterday.

MISSION STATEMENT

My purpose is to honor all those who served in the Vietnam War in the cause of freedom, both Americans and South Vietnamese. My hope is that their sacrifices will not be forgotten and that those who gave their lives in that noble effort to preserve the freedom of the people of the Republic of South Vietnam will be honored for their ultimate sacrifice.

Second, I want to educate people about the Vietnam War so that they have a better understanding about the events of that period. Through my Battle of Kontum website, I hope people will gain insights about that battle and the Vietnam War in general, so they are able to more accurately discern the truthfulness of the narratives from that period.

Third, I hope that this book, "THUNDER Stories From the First Tour," will create for the reader a sense of what it was like to be a combat helicopter pilot during the Vietnam War.

The future belongs to our children and grandchildren. My prayer is that they never have to endure the kind of pain and sacrifice that characterized the Vietnam War years for so many Americans. It is through knowledge and understanding that we grow. Without facing the history that brought us all to where we are now, we will not be able to grow as a people, nor as a person.

Introduction

At one point, a number of years ago, I tried to write a fiction story loosely based on my life experiences. I could never really get into it. I was writing fiction but I kept bumping up against the real story of my experiences. At the time, I was frustrated so I stopped the effort and never went back to it. I always felt that with fiction, I was creating the stories and events rather than revealing the stories and events. In writing this book, I see myself more as a sculptor who chips away the stone to reveal the statue than as a painter who puts paint on a canvas which creates the picture.

Writing about my first tour in Vietnam was never in my plan. The memories and emotions associated with that time in my life were too raw to even look at. I was, however, able to handle writing about the experiences of my second tour in Vietnam, which involved the Easter Offensive and the Battle of Kontum in the spring of 1972. I launched the Battle of Kontum website on March 30, 2002, the 30th anniversary of the battle.

It was a very emotional and painful effort for me and there were many days when my wife would see me reduced to tears as I labored over the story of the Battle of Kontum. It took years for me to be able to face those memories again and write about them. I never felt ready to do that with the first tour memories. Too painful ... just too painful.

I believe all of us must confront our ghosts and deal with the pain, no matter what the source of that pain. Easy to say, hard to do. For combat veterans, I think it is essential to their mental and physical health to deal with their war memories. One of the strategies that helped me was to write about it. The writing of the Battle of Kontum website was a healing activity for me — very cathartic, which helped me greatly with the grieving process. Now I have finally arrived at a place that I can write about my first tour experiences. As I approach my 75th birthday in August 2018, it has been 50 years since my 1967-1968 Vietnam tour.

My motivation to write this book was mostly my need to tell the stories and my children's request to hear the stories. For many years I could do neither. I have found this effort surprising in that the white-hot emotions and storms of my soul have largely subsided, allowing me to be much more objective about those experiences. Because I have retained stacks of my military records over the years, I have had a source to look at for objective evidence, especially on the timing of events, and in some cases, objective "witness" statements that describe specific events.

Late in my career, I received a notice from the Army Personnel Office that they had converted all my official personnel records to an electronic format and that they were going to destroy all the paper files. They gave me the option to request that those files be sent to me. There may have been some small shipping fee I had to pay; I don't remember now. I requested all of them and in a few weeks they came in a cardboard box. Those records have been enormously helpful in writing this book, "Thunder Stories From the First Tour."

The military issued orders for almost everything that we did during our time in the service. For me, that was a career lasting 20 years and seven months. I have stacks of copies of orders that date all the way back to my ROTC college days at Providence College. I have every Officer Efficiency Report (OER) written on me from day one in the Army. I have every letter of commendation and every award citation I ever received. I have my entire history of flight records, all the way back to, and including, my flight school training. I have every academic transcript I ever received, both for my military as well as my civilian education. In a file drawer, there are about 2 feet of military files I have retained.

Writing about my experiences of 50 years ago has been a challenging effort for me at many levels. It has been difficult at times not to conflate events from my second tour in Vietnam with those of my first tour. Over the years, some of those experiences can tend to run together. The records helped me parse out the two tours.

Memories linked to highly emotional events tend to be more easily recalled than those that were not. Much of my combat time was a period of high emotional engagement for me which has helped with the clarity of my memories, at least for the events where I was washed with intense emotions. Other times are less easy to recall.

It is often a problem to go back to old memories without recreating the details of the event, which may not accurately reflect the objective reality of the actual event. I have had many combat veterans tell me that they were afraid to write about their time in Vietnam because they just did not trust their memories and they were afraid that if other combat veterans read their story, they felt the truthfulness of their story could be challenged. No one wants to be labeled a liar or a "BS artist." That is a risk I understand, and I know I am taking that risk by writing my stories.

The written records I have helped me immeasurably in checking myself in the telling of the story.

There have been millions of words written about the Vietnam War, many of which are contained in various books written by Vietnam Veterans. Some are fiction and some are meant to be a recounting of their own life experiences. I have read a great many of them. I am always amazed by the level of detail some authors are able to provide of conversations or even detailed political positions they held at that time. I have not been able to do that to any great extent. I think many times people who read those books forget that sometimes they are actually reading fiction.

There are a few conversations that I remember in a good bit of detail because of the nature of the emotions I was feeling at the time, and I hope I have reproduced them fairly and accurately, if not with the precision of a tape recording or a transcript. If the words are not exact, I believe the gist of the conversation is accurate. I cannot put quotes around any of those conversations.

I have tried to provide enough specificity in the telling of the story that the reader is able to understand the events without going into the minutia of my everyday existence, which would overwhelm the reader and may cloud the picture with unnecessary detail. Striking the balance of enough and not too much has been a challenge. I hope I have achieved that balance.

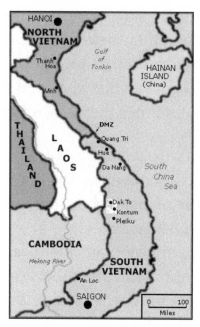

Vietnam War Orientation Map

This map, created by my webmaster, George S. Williams, for my Battle of Kontum website, provides an orientation to where the battle area for me was in 1967-1968 relative to the country of South Vietnam and the adjacent countries of Laos and Cambodia. The battle area, in Kontum Provence, shown as a white rectangle, was about 240 miles north of Saigon and adjacent to Cambodia and Laos. This area was often referred to as the "Tri-border Area" and was the scene of many battles during the Vietnam War, both for the Americans and, at an earlier time, the French. The "Ho Chi Minh Trail" passed just west of this area as it came down through Laos and Cambodia. The battle area was about 60 miles north-to-south and about 40 miles east-to-west, approximately the size of the state of Rhode Island. The city of Pleiku is about 25 miles south of Kontum City. We measured distance more in terms of flight time than actual miles. In a helicopter, I could leave Camp Holloway in Pleiku and be at Kontum City in about 20 minutes.

Acknowledgements

None of us who served in Vietnam can say we did it alone. It was always a team / crew / unit effort. I owe a great deal of gratitude, if not my life, to the brave professionals, both officer and enlisted, who served with me, especially in the 119th Assault Helicopter Company. Their deeds were the measure of who they were and without a doubt, they were all heroes. This book is dedicated to all of them.

My wife, Jean, has always been honest, direct and helpful reviewing anything I have shared with her that I had written. In the writing of this book, she has been helpful in clarifying and filling in some gaps, especially about the times we were together.

Without the experience of telling the story of the

1972 Battle of Kontum on my website, which was the story of my second tour, I would not have been able to write this book about my first tour. Without the genius and dedication of my webmaster George S.Williams, I would never have been able to build and launch that website. The Battle of Kontum website has been visited by millions and represents my effort to honor those who gave their all for our country in a battle most Americans have never heard of.

Finally, a special thanks to my editor, Jeff Pieters, who did yeoman work on my manuscript. I met Jeff through his wife, Joy, who is the daughter of a longtime colleague and friend, Toni Bennett.

CHAPTER 1

The Long Journey To Vietnam

I HAVE HAD a lifelong passion for cars, planes and machines that started early in my life. The first time I was aware of a vehicle, I was eight years old and our family was moving from Slatersville, R.I., to Warwick, R.I. It was a large moving truck with two men in it, taking everything we had to our new home at 413 Long St. in Warwick. My father let me ride with the movers. I sat between them in the cab. It was only about 40 miles, but it seemed like a very long way to me. I remember the roar of the engine and the way the driver shifted gears. As we drove along, the truck just seemed amazing to me. Sitting up there, high in the cab, I felt I was in a very powerful place.

I was the youngest of eight children of Bernard

and Anna Heslin. I was born in Woonsocket Hospital in Rhode Island on Aug. 15, 1943. Dad was an immigrant from Scotland and Mom was second-generation Irish. I was the second boy. My brother was 16 years older than I, and I grew up hardly knowing him. My six older sisters had a big impact on me. As the youngest, and being a boy, I was a bit of a novelty for them. My mother's mother lived with us, and it was clear to me early on that I was Mom's favorite. Between her and my sisters I was on a path to absolute "sissification."

I did not have a close relationship with my father, who was a hard-working chemist in a textile plant. He had bad eyesight as a result of a childhood injury to one of his eyes. That injury kept him out of World War I, but it certainly affected his life. It always fascinated me to know that his livelihood depended on his vision — his ability to examine colors of cloth, and come up with the correct chemical formulas to get the dyes to match.

Dad was an "old school" authoritarian type who believed his responsibility was to bring home a weekly paycheck sufficient to support a family of eight children and a mother-in-law. To his credit, he never failed. I asked him once, when he was in his eighties, what he was most proud of in his life. Without hesitation, he said he was proud of never missing a weekly paycheck. He always turned the money over to his mother-in-law to pay the bills and manage the family finances.

Dad was a strict disciplinarian with a bit of a volatile personality. He believed if you spared the rod, you spoiled the child, so my early years were, at times, painful to my rear end. He was never abusive to any of us, but I clearly remember I was the only one who got spanked. My older sisters, to the best of my memory, never felt his wrath in that fashion.

Dad was 45 years old when I was born, so the age difference had a significant impact on our relationship. He was not the kind of dad who played sports with me or was very involved in my activities, other than to show concern that I did well in school. Dad did his best to support me and would readily spend money for my sports equipment and bikes. I had the best baseball glove and the best bike as a kid.

I loved playing "Army" as a young boy, spending hours with little toy planes, tanks and soldiers. I imagined big battles and sometimes coaxed my older sister into playing with me. Of course, I made up the rules, so I always won, much to the frustration of my sister. I would spend summer days lying on my back in the grass, watching P-51 Mustang fighter planes from the National Guard practicing dogfighting high above our house. Any spare money I could earn was usually spent on model airplanes and other military-style toys or kits to fuel my imagination.

In 1951, when I was 8, my life changed dramatically when my older sister Teresa met Owen Mahony. Owen was a World War II Navy veteran who was older than his peers at Providence College and more mature than most. He courted Teresa for three years. Teresa was four years younger than he was. Owen lived in Woonsocket, R.I., and had only one sibling, a sister. So when he came into my life, I became like his younger brother. For me, he became the most important male figure in my life, playing more the role of father than brother. Ultimately, he made all the difference in my life.

My "sissification" came to an end as I started to model my life after Owen's. He was, without a doubt, my hero and mentor. All the major life decisions in my early years were heavily influenced by him.

Owen was the one who encouraged me to go to La Salle Academy, an all-male Catholic high school that served as a prep school for Providence College. Over my mother's objections, Owen was very supportive of me playing football at La Salle. And La Salle became the stepping stone for me to go to Providence College.

While at Providence, I commuted to school from home as a "day hop." It was less expensive, and I needed to work to pay for my college expenses. I worked as a mechanic in a 64-lane bowling alley on weekends. The Cranston Bowl was managed by my childhood friend Ken Claeson.

During the week, I worked the night shift at the Fruit of the Loom textile plant. Most of the time I drove a forklift. My hours were 5 p.m. to 3 a.m. — 10 hours, four nights a week. It paid well, and I needed the money. There was little

5

time for a social life, but that was OK with me at that time in my life.

I enjoyed the ROTC program and did very well as a student cadet. I achieved the rank of student lieutenant colonel and commanded one of two student battalions. I graduated as a "Distinguished Military Graduate." It was because of my success in the ROTC program that I was offered a regular Army commission upon graduation.

In my junior year of college, there came another life-changing encounter. When I met Jean Savoie, she was a nursing student at the Memorial Hospital School of Nursing, in Pawtucket R.I. We met at a college mixer, and for me, it was love at first sight. Not so much for her, but she eventually came around. We got engaged within six months. I like to think she recognized the potential in me.

Owen was the single person Jean was most concerned to meet when we were dating and anticipating marriage. She knew if she did not meet with Owen's approval, it would not bode well for our relationship. She didn't need to worry.

By the time she met Owen, I was totally in love with her and nothing was going to change that.

As it turned out, Owen saw the same spectacular woman I saw, and he was delighted for us. He wrote a beautiful letter to her which, after more than 50 years, she still has.

Jean was not excited about me going into the military, but we agreed that once I finished my three-year Regular Army (RA) commitment, I could get out without any continuing obligations. My plan was to come out of the military and go back to school to get a master's degree and become a social worker.

On June 1, 1965, I was commissioned a second lieutenant, infantry officer, in the U.S. Army after graduating from Providence's ROTC program. My degree was in sociology, although my real passion was for history. I had, in fact, started college with a history major, but after I almost flunked out my freshman year, I switched to sociology and did much better.

After graduation, I immediately went on two weeks' leave so I could get married to Jean on

June 5, 1965, and take a weeklong honeymoon in Bermuda.

Many people, even family members, advised us not to get married right away — especially since I was going into the Army and had a very uncertain future. Some said I was being unfair to Jean, dragging her away from family and friends with no idea where we were going or what a military life would be like.

I was thankful that my dad was supportive of our choice, and that Jean's parents were also. My mother had reservations, but she was a person of strong faith and she said she would just pray for us. That was what we really needed — support and prayers.

When we returned from the honeymoon, we didn't know it, but Jean was pregnant with our first child. At the time, we had a little black Corvair, and we rented a U-Haul trailer to pull behind it. We loaded all our belongings in the trailer — which looked as big as the car — and drove off one night into the 2 a.m. darkness to my first duty station, the 82nd Airborne Division at Fort Bragg, N.C.

For a couple of 21-year-olds who had hardly been out of Rhode Island, it was a memorable trip that neither of us would ever forget. The adventure had begun.

It was an intense time: adjusting to married life while trying to assimilate into Army culture and an Airborne unit. Fort Bragg was a large Army base, and by June we learned how hot it gets in the South. We were given a small apartment on base and government furniture.

The 82nd had deployed in the spring of 1965 to the Dominican Republic to help put down a communist-inspired revolution. As a result, the only people from the unit still at Fort Bragg were the rear detachments for the various units. I was assigned to the 1st of the 504th Infantry. I was among eight or ten new second lieutenants assigned right out of school to the unit. We had not been to our basic school yet, and we had not gone to jump school to qualify as paratroopers. The derisive term used to describe us was "legs," a name the jump-qualified soldiers loved to use to describe us. We were all anxious to get to jump school as soon as we could, to no longer be "legs."

Because we had not gone to the basic course or jump training, leaders of the unit would not let us go to the Dominican Republic to join the rest of the unit.

Jean was clearly pregnant when we departed Fort Bragg in July to go to Fort Benning, Ga., for me to attend Infantry Officer Basic Course.

Fort Benning at that time was chaotic because the 11th Air Assault Division had been re-designated the 1st Cavalry Airmobile Division and been deployed from Fort Benning to Southeast Asia — Vietnam. This was our first awareness of the war. Some of the wives of the men deployed with the division had been nurses in the local civilian hospital, and their leaving left the hospital short-staffed. When Jean went looking to see if she could get a part-time position, the hospital in Columbus hired her on the spot as a full-time nurse.

For Jean, living in the South was a culture shock. Integration had just happened, and in the hospital it was not going well, as whites and blacks were mixed in wards instead of remaining segregated. Jean has many stressful memories of that period.

After the course was completed, we stayed at Benning so I could go through paratrooper training before returning to Fort Bragg. The 82nd was still in the Dominican Republic (DR), and we knew I would soon be joining them there.

I took Jean home to Rhode Island and left her there with her parents. I deployed to the DR as an infantry platoon leader in the 1st of the 504 infantry, 1/504. My DR experience was hectic, and at times scary, as it was the first time I encountered people who were trying to kill me.

The rear detachment commander for our battalion was a young captain who was getting out of the military. Before I went to Fort Benning, I had performed a number of tasks to help out Capt. Langston. He noted my willingness to help and to do the work. The brigade rear detachment commander, Maj. William P. Grace III, a Vietnam Special Forces veteran, also noted my efforts and work ethic. I did not know at the time I was being watched and talked about.

In December 1965, when Capt. Langston left the Army, it was recommended that I return to Fort Bragg to fill the position of rear detachment commander. It was a significant opportunity for me, because I was only a second lieutenant with very little military experience. I was well thought of for what I did in the DR, and with the recommendation of Maj. Grace and Capt. Langston, my battalion commander, Lt. Col. William "Bill" Bradley and his executive officer, Maj. Wesley R. "Wes" Herrlein, decided to send me back to Bragg. The fact that Jean was late in her pregnancy was something they were aware of, and I think it also influenced their decision.

Just before Christmas of 1965, I returned to Fort Bragg and then went to Rhode Island to pick up Jean. At Bragg, I became the rear detachment commander for the battalion and was responsible for supporting the battalion in the DR and, working stateside, coordinating and facilitating the unit's return to Fort Bragg. It was a challenging position that required me to work long hours, as aircraft from the DR arrived at 4 a.m., and often there were late-evening aircraft departures I had to coordinate and work with. There were significant personnel problems in the Rear Detachment, because soldiers who had been discipline problems in the DR were sent back for me to deal with. That often meant non-judicial action under Article 15 of the Uniform Code of Military Justice or, in some cases, court-martials. There was a constant demand for me to obtain supplies to send to the unit in the DR, from vehicles to all kinds of other supplies.

Jean gave birth to our first child, John, on Feb. 25, 1966. It was a momentous occasion for us — truly life-changing. We were 22 years old, in a fast-moving world with war on the horizon.

During the spring of 1966, a new battalion commander arrived at Fort Bragg. Lt. Col. Day was replacing Lt. Col. William "Bill" Bradley. I had a role in helping Lt. Col. Day in the transition period and developed a friendly relationship with him. During that time, the action in Vietnam was escalating, with the 1st Air Cavalry Division having been deployed in the late summer of 1965. Lt. Col. Day strongly suggested to me that I look into going to flight school, because he believed that Army aviation was the wave of the future.

Jean and I talked about it, and I decided to apply. First I had to take a flight aptitude test. It was a four-hour test, and on the day I was scheduled to take it, there was an emergency in the unit, and I couldn't get to the test site on time. I showed up an hour late. The person administering the test said it was too late; I had missed too much time. I asked if I could take it anyway, and just take whatever result I got. With reluctance, the administrator let me in and I sat down to take the test. I received one of the highest scores of those who took the test, so I qualified. After taking the appropriate medical exam and a brief orientation flight in a helicopter, I submitted the rather voluminous application for flight school.

After several weeks, the entire application package was returned because I had missed filling in a couple of blocks on the form. I'd put a lot of time and effort into that application, and I was disappointed. In fact, I must have been pissed off, because I took the entire package and threw it in the wastebasket.

At that time, I had a wonderful first sergeant named Alley. He was back at Fort Bragg on a compassionate assignment because his wife had been sick.

One day, Sgt. Alley came into my office and said

there was a call for me from the Pentagon. This was unusual. A Lt. Col. Folda was on the line. He was the assignment officer for the Army flight program. He said he had my application on his desk and wondered if I wanted fixed wing training (airplanes) or rotary wing training (helicopters). I was shocked. I looked up, and Sgt. Alley was standing in the doorway with a smile on his face. It turned out he had found my application in the trash and completed the forms, signing my name and submitting it without my knowledge.

As for the training choice, I told Lt. Col. Folda it didn't matter to me. I asked, what did the Army need most? He said helicopter pilots. I said that would be great, and he said I would have orders within the next few days assigning me to Fort Wolters, Texas, to attend Rotary Wing flight training. And so, for Jean and me, a new adventure began.

In September 1966, Jean and I left Fort Bragg with our new son and all our possessions in a new maroon 1966 Chevy Malibu, headed to Fort Walters.

At that time, Fort Wolters was one of the largest

flight training bases in the world. Mineral Wells, the town adjacent to the base, was little more than a dilapidated, little southern town full of dirt and dust, known for its mineral baths and a large, decrepit hotel in the middle of town. The town was profiting big time from the influx of Army soldiers going to school there. They were renting anything from chicken coops to absolute shacks. The townspeople knew we had no choice and that we'd take whatever we could get. After some horrible experiences looking at temporary living spaces for the four months we'd spend there, Jean and I found a roach-infested apartment we paid too much for, but it was all that was available. Jean was appalled by the conditions, but she showed her mettle and made it work for us.

On my first day at the flight line, after a wonderful orientation flight in an OH — 23-D with my new, very young civilian instructor, he and the other student took off. A short time later, they crashed near the Brazos River. Both died.

The Army's need to notify the next of kin prevented our wives from finding out who had been killed until we finally got home that night, about

11 p.m. This was a very sobering experience for all of us, now freshly aware of the dangers we were now facing. Jean stood with me in the face of it to continue my training, but after that incident, several other students dropped out.

I showed up the next day for training and, after meeting my new instructor, Mr. Vaughn, an older civilian instructor pilot, along with a new student, I was back in the air to complete my training.

After Fort Wolters, we went to Fort Rucker in Enterprise, Ala., for the final phase of training. We flew the new UH — 1 helicopters. It was challenging and exhilarating as we pressed the envelope of our skills and mental abilities. We did instrument training, tactical flight training and cross-country navigation. All along the way, we had to pass flight tests with our instructor pilots and a wide range of academic tests. Failure was not an option. If you failed a flight check ride and got a "pink slip," you had one more chance to succeed. If you failed again, you were either washed out of the program or recycled to the next class. These were very stressful times. The training was tough and life with a new baby in a small house without air-conditioning in the summer heat of Alabama was difficult for both me and Jean.

All of us knew that when we graduated we would be deployed to Vietnam. Jean and I made close friends during those flight school days, and several of those friendships have lasted more than 50 years now. While we were at Fort Rucker, Jean gave birth to our second child, Joan, on May 4, 1967.

Upon graduation, I was assigned back to Fort Bragg to be part of a new assault helicopter company (AHC) forming up to go to Vietnam in the fall of 1967. The 57th AHC was top-heavy with rank, as many longtime fixed-wing aviators had transitioned to helicopters and were filling the new units deploying. As a result, as a first lieutenant, I was just a pilot in a platoon with no responsibilities other than to fly an aircraft. All the leadership positions were filled with senior captains and majors.

After bringing Jean back to Rhode Island with our son and new daughter, and putting them all in a rental house, I returned to Fort Bragg and joined the unit as we flew our fleet of helicopters cross-country to Sharp Army Depot near San Francisco. It was an amazing trip with a number of overnight stops along the way. My flight records indicate that the flight took place from Sept. 3-8, and that I flew a total of 25.3 hours.

At the time, neither Jean nor I were aware that Jean was pregnant with our third child.

With the aircraft on the way to Vietnam by ship, we were allowed to take a short leave before deploying as a unit out of Fort Bragg on Air Force C-141 jet cargo planes that took us directly into Pleiku, South Vietnam, in the highlands of II Corps.

WELCOME TO VIETNAM.

CHAPTER 2

The Silver Bullet

NOTHING PREPARED ME for the absolutely devastating heat that greeted us as we stepped out off the plane onto the tarmac of the Pleiku airfield. It was Oct. 21 and the Highlands was just coming out of the rainy season.

We were put on trucks and taken about five miles south of the airbase to an Army base in Pleiku called Camp Holloway, named in 1963 for a CH-21 helicopter pilot, Warrant Officer Charles E. Holloway, who in December 1962 became the first Army aviator from the 81st Transportation Company to be killed in action.

I will never forget the intensity of the heat and the general feeling of confusion as we were bundled into a sort of tent camp on the side of the Holloway airstrip to await the next step in the process. That first night at Holloway was an anxious one. There were reports that Holloway was going to come under attack that night. We were packed into tents with no way to defend ourselves if the Viet Cong (VC) penetrated the perimeter wire. We only had our sidearms, our Army-issued .38-caliber revolvers, but we had not been issued ammunition. One of the guys had brought a box of .38 ammunition he had bought on the economy before we left Fort Bragg. He gave each of us one bullet — a silver bullet with a lead tip. We all speculated what we would do with our one bullet if the hordes came to overrun us. I have that bullet to this day.

The first night passed without incident, other than some distant explosions and flares fired from the camp's 81 mm mortars.

Early the next day, an officer came through the area. I think he was a captain. He had some paperwork in his hand and was asking for volunteers to be "infused" into an existing unit at Camp Holloway.

When new units came into Vietnam, the policy

was to take at least one-third of the officers and reassign them to a unit that had been there for a while, and have the more experienced people take their place, so the new unit would have experienced folks to help bring the unit up to speed. It also served to prevent a situation where all the members of the new unit would be rotating out to go home — we called it DEROS — at the same time after the one-year deployment.

I stopped the captain and asked which unit he was recruiting for, and what was the job or assignment in that unit. He told me he was putting people in the 119th AHC at Camp Holloway and that he had a platoon commander position available. At the time, I was just a UH-1 pilot in one of the 57th lift platoons with little prospects for moving up in responsibility. I told him I wanted to go and would love to get the job as a platoon commander, so he took my name and told me to pack up my stuff and report to the 119th orderly room for assignment.

Some of my friends were shocked that I would so quickly be willing to leave them and go to another unit, but I saw it as a case where I would have a chance to have a challenging job so, while I would miss my friends, I saw the move as the best option for me.

The 57th AHC was scheduled to move up to the airfield at Kontum, about 40 to 50 km north of Pleiku. That was pretty much all we knew at the time. It turned out to be a very fortuitous choice for me as the one-year combat tour unfolded.

CHAPTER **3**

"Blue One"

WHEN I SIGNED into the 119th, after meeting the company commander, I was introduced to the current platoon commander, Capt. Sid Richardson, of the 1st lift platoon, known as the "Blue" platoon. There were two lift platoons in an Assault Helicopter Company (AHC) — the Blue platoon and the Yellow platoon. As the Blue platoon commander, you had a call sign of "Blue One." Flying missions, when we communicated over the radio we usually used our call signs to identify ourselves.

Sid Richardson was "Blue One" and I was his replacement, or "turtle." I would go through in-country orientation and aircraft checkouts before I assumed the duties of the platoon commander.

This was late October and the weather in the Highlands was getting better as the dry season was moving in. I remember getting all the personal equipment I would be flying with, including a personal weapon. I turned in the .38 and got a .45-caliber automatic, also known as a 1911.

In a UH-1 helicopter, the pilots sat in armored seats. The part of the seat you sat on was a nylon mesh fabric. If the aircraft took a hit under the seat, it was like being spanked very hard, but if the bullet didn't penetrate the armor, there was no blood, as they say. The only other place on the aircraft that had an armor shield was over the oil cooler, just below the engine. If we lost our oil cooler, it would quickly cause the engine to fail.

I was able to get an AR-15, or CAR, instead of the standard M-16 rifle. I liked the CAR because, while it fired the same magazine and bullets as the M-16, it was much shorter and easier to handle in confined spaces. I also purchased a western style holster for my pistol, which hung low on my hip and had a place for an extra magazine. Putting the holster between my legs with the .45 in it gave me a false sense of security that it could save my balls. Glad it never got tested with me.

I was issued a ceramic bulletproof breastplate and flak vest. On top of all that, I wore an Air Force-type survival vest with all the necessary stuff in it, including an ARC-10 UHF survival radio. We all had steel helmets as well as our flight helmets, and on this first tour we wore jungle fatigues and jungle boots. It was not until my second tour that we had fire-retardant Nomex two-piece flight suits.

I moved into one of the Blue platoon billets, a tin-and-canvas type building with sandbags stacked around it. It was little more than a tent but it did have a tin roof, which tended to keep the rain out better than just canvas. Located more or less in the center of Camp Holloway, we had a pretty good walk to the flight line, which for the 119th was called the Swamp. The 119th company call sign, which was also used for the UH-1 lift platoons, was the Alligators or "Gators," and the 119th UH —1C gunship platoon was known as the Crocodiles or just the "Crocs."

We were all assigned defensive positions along the perimeter, a series of trenches and sandbag bunkers that we would occupy at night if we were attacked, or if an enemy attack was threatened. Think about sleeping in mud and you have it about right.

Not long after arriving in the unit, I was assigned an orientation mission in a UH-1 helicopter, also known as a "slick," as opposed to the UH-1C gunships, known simply as the "guns." This would be more of an administrative mission than a combat assault mission. The intent of this first mission was for me to become familiar with the local flying area and some of the procedures and policies of the unit. Until I qualified as an aircraft commander, I would fly as a pilot. For that first flight, the aircraft commander was a young warrant officer named Miller, whom I met at the aircraft for the preflight brief and preflight aircraft inspection. I remember looking at that young man who was getting close to the end of his tour, thinking he looked like a kid. But as I looked closer, into his eyes, he appeared more like an old man. It was a sight I have never forgotten, and as my tour unfolded, I understood how young kids became old men in the white-hot fire of almost daily combat flying.

I quickly accumulated combat flight hours in support of American units involved with big battles in the vicinity of the Ia Drang Valley and in the mountains around Dak To. The Ia Drang Valley was famous for the first big American battles in November 1965, when units of the 1st Cavalry Division faced a large, determined North Vietnamese unit in a costly three-day battle at a place called "LZ Xray." The movie "We Were Soldiers" starring Mel Gibson and based on the book "We Were Soldiers Once … and Young," by Lt. Gen. Harold G. "Hal" Moore and Joseph L. Galloway, provided a detailed, realistic picture of that battle, by this time two years past.

As part of our in-country orientation, all the new pilots were told we were restricted to flying no more than 90 hours in a 30-day period. If we needed to exceed that, we had to see the flight surgeon, who could authorize us to fly a maximum of 110 hours in 30 days. I have copies of my original flight records from Vietnam, which show that in the first 30 days of flying, Oct. 25 to Nov. 25, I flew 147 hours, and by Nov. 30 I had flown 163.5 hours. I do not remember ever talking to a flight surgeon.

During that late October and early November period, I was flying almost daily in support of combat operations of the 4th Infantry Division, which was fighting the battle of Dak To, north of Pleiku in Kontum Province. The 4th Infantry Division was based at Camp Enari, a large, sprawling base about 10 km south of Camp Holloway. The base was named for 1st Lt. Mark Enari, the first 4th Infantry Division member awarded the Silver Star (posthumously) in Vietnam. He had been KIA on Dec. 2, 1966.

The predominant land feature near Camp Enari was a large mountain mass that rose up out of the plateau area around Pleiku Province. It was known as "Dragon Mountain" and also "Titty Mountain" because of its shape. The mountain was littered with aircraft wrecks. In bad weather or at night, the mountain claimed many lives.

The 4th Division had its own combat aviation battalion with liftships and gunships. My friend from flight school, Dan Baker, was assigned to the gun platoon at the same time I was with the

119th. He was shot down one day near the Ia Drang while covering a combat assault. Dan was sent to the 71st Evac hospital in Pleiku with non-life threatening injuries and was eventually medically evacuated back to the States. He did not stay in the military long after that.

The 119th was one of three assault helicopter companies (AHC) assigned to Camp Holloway. The other two, the 170th AHC with a call sign of "Bikini" and the 189th AHC with a call sign of "Ghost Rider," were, like the 119th, in general support rather than assigned directly to a division. There was also the 179th CH-47 Chinook Medium Lift Helicopter Company with a call sign of "Shrimpboats." There were also a number of maintenance units and other support units on base.

The battalion headquarters for the 52nd Combat Aviation Battalion, which was our senior headquarters, was also located at Holloway. At that time, I think there was a total of about 1,500 troops on the base.

CHAPTER **4**

Taking It Through The Trees

WE WERE ALL putting in long hours during the battle of Dak To in late October and November of 1967. I remember coming back to base one day, and on my cot was a set of captain's bars. I did not know until then that I had been promoted to the rank of captain on Nov. 1.

Most of the flying at that time was combat assault flying. On a daily basis we were putting troops in the landing zones (LZs) in the mountains around Dak To. It was extremely difficult flying.

We were flying combat assault missions that required early takeoff and we flew numerous missions inserting troops in remote LZs — which often became hot LZs as the enemy fought back with intense ground fire. As the day progressed, we were often medevacking wounded soldiers and flying in much-needed water and ammunition. Aircraft being hit by ground fire was common, and many times helicopters were shot down, landing in the jungle in a horrendous mess of twisted metal and slashing blades. In those days, we did not have crash-worthy fuel systems, so an aircraft shot down often turned into a big orange ball of burning metal. A large cloud of black smoke coming up out of the jungle was a sure sign that a helicopter had just crashed there. Burning up in an aircraft was a fear we all lived with, and if you ever saw the results of that, you would never forget it. I haven't.

At the end of the day, which often ended up in darkness, we would bring in water, ammunition and C-rations to the infantry units we had put in earlier in the day.

On one of those late-in-the-day missions, we were hauling a load of C-rations to a battalion in the field. The crew chief loaded all the boxes of C's he could fit into the cargo area of our Huey. When I lifted the helicopter to a hover, I noticed that I had to hold the cyclic control well back toward my seat more than usual, but I figured it was just because of the heavy load, and so off we went to the unit in the field. The LZ was located over a large ridgeline south of Dak To, and it was not much more than a hover hole.

I made a shallow approach to the LZ because the trees on the approach side were relatively small, but I could see the trees in the back of the LZ were tall and thick. As I slowed the aircraft down to come to a hover, I was shocked to find that I was banging the cyclic control against my seat and the aircraft was not stopping its forward movement. We were going to crash into the trees at the far end of the LZ if I could not stop the aircraft. In an instant, I realized that the heavy weight of the C-ration boxes, along with my low fuel situation, had seriously changed the center of balance of the aircraft and we were well out of our normal limits in a nose-low attitude.

The only choice I had was to pull in as much power as I could and try to fly over the trees. Everything seemed to go in slow motion as we approached the trees. At the last minute, I could see a break between the trees that would allow me to fly the body of the aircraft through, but not the main rotor blades. As we passed through the break, branches were banging against our windshield and the cabin, but miraculously the main rotor blades just barely cleared the treetops and we literally flew through the trees. Once out, we could gain airspeed and slowly climb to altitude in a very nose-low attitude.

We headed for the airstrip at Dak To and made a "run-on" landing, which meant we landed much the same as a fixed-wing aircraft, sliding on our skids. As soon as we got the helicopter stopped, the crew chief and gunner pulled all the boxes of C's out of the cabin and, with that, we could hover over to the fuel point and top off with fuel.

When we had a full tank of fuel, the weight of it brought our center of gravity back into normal range, so we reloaded about half of the C's, making two trips to the field unit rather than trying to do it all in one load. If I had plowed into the trees that day, the death and destruction that would have resulted would have been for one reason and one reason only: pilot error.

Usually the last thing we did after a day of supporting troops in the field was to backhaul the dead. The dead bodies might be in body bags, if the units had them available and had the time to use them, or they would just put the bodies in the aircraft as quickly as they could, sometimes wrapped in ponchos. That could include badly torn-up bodies or pieces of bodies. Those memories do not ever go away.

In the period of Nov. 2 to 23, 1967, the battles in the mountains around Dak To and out near the Cambodia-Laos border were fierce. Because I was not yet an aircraft commander (AC), I flew in the right seat of the helicopter and logged time as the pilot. The aircraft commander always flew in the left seat of a UH-1 (Huey) helicopter and logged AC time, which was considered the same as pilot time rather than co-pilot time. The AC was the absolute authority on the aircraft no matter what rank he held. Many times, senior officers flew as pilot where the AC was a warrant officer. You could not fly or log time as an AC until you qualified and received orders designating you as an AC.

Army aviation has always been built on a combination of commissioned officers and warrant officers. Most of the flight slots in any aviation unit were filled by warrant officers, whose primary job was to fly. The commissioned officers, who comprised about 15 percent of an Army aviation unit, filled command and staff positions and flew aircraft as pilots as a secondary duty. For example, I was first and foremost an infantry officer with a secondary military occupation specialty as a pilot. This dual-hatting of commissioned officers caused a considerable stress on the individual officers to maintain proficiency in two different specialties.

On one of our missions, when a 4th Division battalion had taken many casualties up on the ridge line south of Dak To, I went in to bring water and ammunition and to back haul dead. There were a lot of them. The period of late 1967 and early 1968 had some of the most intense fighting for American units in the entire war. Hundreds were dying every week. As I approached the general location of the LZ, we couldn't find it. After a number of radio calls with the ground unit popping smoke a number of times, we finally saw red smoke drifting up through the jungle canopy. It was important to identify the color smoke, because the enemy often would pop smoke to confuse us.

We circled around the treetops to find an opening in the canopy to go in. The trees were 150 to 200 feet high. I was flying in the right seat as pilot. The AC that day was a young warrant officer. My hands were on the controls as we let down very slowly through a hole in the canopy. It was the most intense flying I had ever done up to that point. I'd graduated from flight school with top grades for my flying ability, but nothing had prepared me for this kind of combat flying. It was at the extreme edge of my abilities and the capability of the Huey aircraft we were flying.

As we let down through the tree branches, our crew chief and door gunner were constantly giving us guidance over the aircraft intercom system with precise directions such as "down two feet, now slide left three feet and come down 10 feet." While they were giving directions, we had to listen to as many as four onboard radios: two FM radios, a VHF radio and a UHF. Usually the ground unit was on one or two of the FM frequencies, our gunships normally operated on VHF frequencies and our Air Force forward air controllers (FACs) were on UHF frequencies. The UHF frequencies were also for the emergency radio channel. If an aircraft was hit and going down, the pilot would send out his "Mayday" call over the UHF emergency channel. We always listened to the UHF "guard" channel. Add to that the communications in the cockpit among the four crew members, and just sorting it all out was very difficult, especially when voices got loud and frantic with the stress of combat.

Eventually we got down to the LZ, which was nothing but a hover hole. Once in it, you couldn't see the sky if you looked up through the overhead window. As I made my final descent, I was focused on one thing on the ground below me as a point of reference. I couldn't make out what it was because it kept flapping around in my rotor wash. As the thing became clearer to me, I realized I was looking at a soldier's severed head that had been split open. I have never forgotten that sight.

As we hovered in the LZ, we pushed off the water and ammunition we had brought with us. The unit started to load us up with their dead. There was a large stack of bodies beside the little LZ. I don't remember how many we took out that time, but it took a while to load them, and some of the dead were in bits and pieces. None of them were in body bags and only a few of them were wrapped in their ponchos. I remember at one point reaching down to my radio panel to change frequencies and having to move a severed arm that was lying across the panel. Those memories never go away.

After being loaded up, we started back up through the trees with the same precise instructions from the crew that had brought us down. It was extremely tense and I remember I was controlling the aircraft with just the tips of my fingers. It was as if just thinking of what control input was needed was all I had to do. Anyone looking at my hands would have seen them barely moving.

Once safely out of the hole, we headed back to the Dak To airstrip, where a field morgue had been set up to offload the bodies. After refueling, we went out and did it again and again until I felt numb.

There was also a field hospital, a MASH, beside the runway at Dak To, working hard 24/7. We often had missions to take the wounded from the MASH and bring them to Pleiku, about 70 to

80 km south, where the 71st Evacuation Hospital was located. The 71st Evac was much better staffed and equipped than the field MASH.

CHAPTER 5

The Dog Bone

ON ONE OF those missions during the Battle of Dak To — and I lost track of how many there were, or even how many days we were doing that, they all ran together — we got a mayday call on the UHF guard radio channel. It was from an Air Force FAC who was hit and was going to parachute out of his burning aircraft. I believe it was in mid-November.

The pilot said he was south of Dak To, over the valley where there was a 4th Division Fire Support Base (FSB) that we called the "Dog Bone," because from the air it looked like a giant dog bone. We all knew where it was.

We had been part of a combat assault mission with a number of other helicopters at the time.

When we heard the "mayday" call we were not far from the Dog Bone, so we started looking for the parachute. Off in the distance we saw it, with the pilot hung below. It was not far from the FSB, but not so close that the pilot would have been easy to reach from the ground. It was clear that where he was going to land would be very close to enemy units, if not on top of them. As the chute descended to the ground, we could see it land in a large area of bamboo grass and trees. The chute was clearly visible but we could no longer see the pilot down in the bamboo.

When we got closer, the pilot came up on his ARC 10 emergency UHF radio. We all carried ARC 10s in our survival vests for this very reason. He was very excited and was desperately trying to make contact. We answered his call, much to his relief. We told him that we saw his chute but couldn't see him. He said he was not far from the chute. We knew time was of the essence because we were sure the enemy would try to capture the pilot as quickly as they could. There was just no time to waste, and it was very fortunate that we were so close and saw him come down.

We told him as we flew over him to call "bingo" to indicate we were overhead. It wasn't long before we heard "bingo, bingo, bingo." Unfortunately, the bamboo was very thick and none of us could see the pilot. The situation was getting desperate, and I decided we would take a chance on the thickness of the bamboo. We slowly flew over until we heard "bingo" again. We came to a hover. The bamboo was blowing around in the rotor wash, and the door gunner caught a glimpse of the pilot below us. I lowered the collective control of the aircraft so we could descend into the bamboo. At that moment I did not know if our main rotor blades would be able to cut their way down or if we would lose it in the trees.

As I slowly descended, the door gunner climbed out onto the skid to reach down for the pilot's hand. At that point, bamboo was flying everywhere. We got low enough to reach the pilot, and the door gunner was able to pull him into the aircraft. I remember looking over my shoulder to see one very big smile on a happy Air Force pilot. We went back up out of the bamboo and took him to safety at the Dak To airstrip.

After we dropped him off, we went over to the fuel area and shut the aircraft down to assess the damage. After inspecting the blades and the rest of the aircraft, we all decided we were fine, so we cranked the helicopter back up and went out to rejoin the other aircraft.

I never learned the name of the pilot and I am sure he never learned our names. We did what any other helicopter crew would have done. There was talk of medals for the rescue, but nothing ever came of it. When we got back to base that night, we made an entry in the aircraft log book so maintenance could check the air-craft more closely.

CHAPTER 6

SOG

IN EARLY NOVEMBER, I was getting ready to replace Sid Richardson as the platoon commander because he was scheduled to go home in December. We called that date your DEROS date, which was your departure date from Vietnam. DEROS stood for Date Eligible for Return from Overseas. Sometime during the third week of November, Sid came to me and said that I needed to pack up my stuff and fly up to a Special Forces compound just south of Kontum, known as Forward Operating Base 2 (FOB 2). He said I would be flying with the 189th Ghost Riders for a week so I could become familiar with the mission before my platoon joined me at the FOB on Dec. 1. We were scheduled to support the Special Forces (SF) mission out of FOB 2, known as SOG, for a two-month cycle beginning on Dec. 1. Sid said I would be briefed on the details of the mission when I arrived at the FOB. I was going to stay at the compound and support the mission through the end of January 1968.

Big surprise. The mission was, at the time, a top-secret mission involved to insert small reconnaissance teams deep inside Laos and Cambodia. SOG stood for Studies and Observation Group, which was a cover name for the top secret Special Forces mission along the Ho Chi Minh Trail.

The Special Forces SOG mission operating out of FOB 2 in Kontum was under the control of Command and Control Central, or just CCC. It was one of the Military Assistance Command Vietnam — SOG (MACV-SOG) operations, which also had similar SOG units operating in the southern part of South Vietnam and also in the northern part of South Vietnam. The missions that went into Laos had a code name of "Shining Brass" and later "Prairie Fire." There was also a code name for SOG missions run into Cambodia, initially "Daniel Boone" and later "Salem House."

When I was first at the FOB, there was an emphasis on trying to be secretive and not appear to the enemy as a U.S. unit. I think they were trying for plausible denial of some type. Even at that time, I did not think that was possible.

The SOG mission was considered top secret and we all had to sign documents stating that we would never reveal what we did on the mission or talk about it with anyone. We could not even talk to other aviators in Vietnam about the mission. There was a sense of total secrecy.

I kept the mission to myself for many years, not even telling my wife what we did until John Plaster published his book "SOG: The Secret Wars of America's Commandos in Vietnam" in 1997. I was stunned when it first appeared. I bought a copy and stayed up all night reading about things I knew about and had done. I knew many of the names, places and events that John had in his book. Later, when the SOG mission got the Presidential Unit Citation in 2001, it was all out in the public press for everyone to know what we did. It is an extraordinary story of courage and determination by a very small group of men. It is a story most Americans have never heard of.

At times, the SOG command would launch assault units made up of 35 to 40 men, who would conduct raids along the Trail. They were called Hornet Forces or companies.

Most of the time there were small recon teams, named after states and led by American Special Forces personnel, usually noncommissioned officers. Most of the time there were two Americans and the remainder of the team was made up of Montagnards. The Montagnards were mountain tribal men who lived in Kontum Province.

For the remainder of November, I flew with the 189th flight platoon commander, 1st Lt. Stephen R. Schmidt. It was a very intense mission, with many aircraft suffering combat damage. The mission required a full 10-ship UH-1H platoon and 6 to 8 UH-1C gunships. All the aircraft staged out of the FOB and the crews lived on the compound among the SF personnel. As a result, the air crews became close to the SF men they were supporting. The compound provided for its own defense with perimeter bunkers and mortars.

There was a small building that served as a sort of all-ranks club. It was clearly a place for those assigned to the FOB to unwind and, for some, to get totally blown away with alcohol. Fights were not uncommon and behavior of the SF soldiers could, at times, be bizarre. Although I did not drink much alcohol during my first tour in Vietnam, I did enjoy going to the little club at night for the comradery and to hear the many war stories shared by the SOG men of missions they had been on.

The daily mission briefs took place in a small underground bunker where the flight leader and team leader would get briefed on the next day's mission. Orders and priorities for the missions came down from the highest authorities in Saigon, and sometimes even higher authority. They often signaled great urgency, such as capturing a North Vietnamese Army (NVA) truck driver from his truck as he drove down the Ho Chi Minh Trail and bringing him back alive. It happened; they did it.

The lift platoon commander functioned as the air mission commander and often was also the flight lead. During my time flying with the 189th, I became very familiar with the mission and was prepared to assume the role of air mission commander when my platoon arrived from Camp Holloway on Dec. 1.

While flying with the 189th, I was involved with a number of insertions and extractions of small recon teams in both Laos and Cambodia. When flying in Laos, we could call for and get a very high priority for close air support from Air Force, Navy and Marines fixed-wing fighter bombers. When we flew in Cambodia, we were not able to get close air support because of political restrictions that prevented them from entering Cambodian airspace. As reported by many, the politics of that war cost many American lives.

The SOG mission folks always had one of their team members in the forward air control (FAC) aircraft operating in support of the mission. Their call sign was "Covey." These FAC aircraft were usually an Army O-1 "Bird Dog," which was a small single-engine spotter plane. Armed only with smoke rockets they could use to mark targets, they had no real attack capability.

When my platoon deployed to the FOB, we replaced the 189th. It was late 1967 and the North Vietnamese were intensifying their efforts to bring men and material down the trail. The US / ARVN command leadership were very concerned because they didn't know why there was such intense activity on the Trail. They knew something big was in the works, but no one knew what it was. Later, in January and February, we would all know — when the large-scale attacks took place across South Vietnam, known as the Tet Offensive of 1968.

The urgency to get information about the build-up along the trail was the highest priority, and it caused an intense effort and increase of operations for the SOG teams at FOB 2. As a result, missions were being conducted almost on a daily basis, both into Laos and Cambodia. The increased activity was noted by the North Vietnamese and they doubled their efforts to defeat the SOG missions.

The bravery of the SOG men was nothing short of amazing. I came to know a number of them while on this assignment. The SOG unit was one of the most highly decorated units in the Army. It was reported that members of this SOG unit had earned five Medals of Honor. During this period I knew two Medal of Honor recipients:

Sgt. Robert "Bob" Howard, who later got a direct commission and eventually retired as a full colonel, and Sgt. Fred Zabitosky. Bob Howard was one of the most highly decorated soldiers in the Vietnam War. Fred had a major street at Fort Bragg named after him.

Another member of the SOG team at that time was Sgt. Johnny Gilreath, who, like Bob Howard and Fred Zabitosky, did amazing things as a SOG team leader. I remember Johnny told me he wanted to become a pilot. I was told that Johnny eventually went to flight school and became an Army aviator. I have many memories of other members of the SOG team, both enlisted and officers.

The SOG unit was awarded the Presidential Unit Citation at Fort Bragg, N.C., on April 4, 2001. The Citation covered the period from Jan. 24, 1964, through April 30, 1972. It was interesting to me to have been with SOG in 1967 and 1968 and then to be back there in April 1972 when they stood down. In May 1972, after the SOG mission was stood down, I flew into the old FOB camp in my OH-58 to get fuel during the 1972 Battle of Kontum — but that is another story.

It would be impossible for me to recall all the details of the many missions I flew during that period. There are a few, however, that stand out in my memory, and some that I have witness statements on that I have used here for accuracy. Other stories are from the best of my ability to recall.

CHAPTER 7

The Hornet Force

ONE OF THE missions I flew with the 189th involved extracting a large team from a hot LZ in Laos. My flying skills were above average, so I was often on the controls when we went into a tight or hot LZ. I was awarded the Air Medal with "V" device for heroism for action on Nov. 27, 1967. The mission involved flying into a very small LZ to extract wounded soldiers while we were under intense enemy fire. We succeeded in getting the wounded out. The other pilot with me was the platoon commander, 1st Lt. Stephen R. Schmidt, from the 189th AHC, and he was awarded the Distinguished Flying Cross.

Here is a description of the ground action from the SOG men during that mission. This witness statement was used for approving the various awards associated with the action. (This statement has been reproduced exactly as the original, signed copy that I have in my files.)

"On the morning of 27 November 1967, I was in a perimeter deep in enemy territory as directed by the 5th Special Forces. We had been in contact continuously and had called for an emergency extraction. The extraction was to be from a position west of Dak To, deep in the jungles out of range of supporting artillery. The unit to be extracted was an 80 man force that had been inserted the day previous. We had two killed and four wounded the previous day. An aircraft from the 189th Aviation Company had attempted to extract the wounded the previous evening and had received twelve hits with the Aircraft Commander (AC) receiving multiple serious wounds requiring evacuation and the pilot receiving one leg wound. The aircraft received battle damage of sufficient magnitude to require major repair work. The attempted extraction was preceded by a close air strike by an A-1E aircraft controlled by a FAC. The jungle canopy was too thick to permit even limited observation from more than 500 feet actual altitude. The 80 man force was unable to move from the bomb crater in the midst of 120 foot trees where it was pinned down at the time of the extraction. The unit was running low on ammunition and had run out of water. The situation was critical. I saw the flight from the 189th Avn. Co. arrive. They began an orbit out of sight from my position. By this time six more of the 80 man force were wounded. Sporadic fire was being received from three quadrants. Light mist surrounded the area which I later found out would force the rescuing aircraft to use a twisting route to reach the LZ which was invisible from altitude as it was extremely small and surrounded by jungle.

Upon arrival MAJ Sanders made contact

with this unit and requested smoke. He began a low level orbit to check for enemy troops, and to locate the LZ. He saw our smoke coming out of what appeared to be the middle of the jungle but later proved to be our hole in the jungle made by a bomb crater. It did not appear to me to be large enough to permit a helicopter to land. I later found that it allowed two foot clearance for the blade and the tail could be jockeyed down through the canopy. We continued to report firing and the four gunships with CPT Hooper, WO Jones, WO Durham, and WO Ginac as aircraft commanders, WO Butler, Wo Ochotsky, WO Kreutz, and WO Webster as pilots, PFC Leburn, SP5 Shooships, SP4 Tipton, and SP5 Schenk as crew chief/gunners, and SP4 Buchanan, SP5 Tillman, SP4 Williams, and SP4 Reigadas as gunners began firing runs to relieve pressure from our encircled troops. The firing runs were made at extreme low level to enable observation of effect as well as to evaluate the threat. From my position it appeared that they grazed the tree tops. These low level runs were made with the full knowledge that a well armed and determined enemy was at that position. The firing passes were of such extreme accuracy and brought so close to our defending friendly troops that the threat of being overrun was virtually eliminated. The gun ships continued to fly low level passes to draw fire and thereby locate the hidden enemy. The mission commander continued to orbit above the site. MAJ Sanders directed the first UH-1H in. The LZ was again marked by smoke but because of its small size and the high jungle canopy could not be located by the "slick". MAJ Sanders dropped to approximately 500 feet absolute altitude and orbited over the ringed LZ, calmly directing the slicks into the LZ. I shall describe the approach as I saw it from the ground. This description must be said for every other approach and departure. The slick came from the East as all other quadrants, in spite of a tremendously accurate volume of fire from the gun ships, were occupied by an emplaced enemy who was delivering a significant amount of small arms and automatic weapons fire throughout the engagement. The approach was through wisps of fog above the tree tops. In all landings except that of the C&C ship direction and vectoring was received from the C&C ship. The smoke from the LZ was barely visible. As it was invariably thinned after having risen 100 to 120 feet through the canopy. The ship arrived over the LZ which was a bomb crater that had destroyed some small trees. Some demolition had created a frying pan effect with the handle pointed west so the aircraft had to come to a hover at the LZ at 120 feet facing east, perform a pedal turn and snake down into the LZ. All members of the crew were actively assisting the A/C by directing turn left or right to clear the tail rotor and main rotor blades through the confined column down to a one foot hover. (The ground was badly contoured by the bomb and to set down the skids would result in loss of the aircraft). While the A/C and pilots held the aircraft at a hover the rescued personnel jumped aboard the aircraft. It should be remembered that the area was so confined the 24″ movement to either flank or 48″ movement forward would result in a blade strike and perhaps the loss of the aircraft. The piloting in this situation was flawless. All the while fire from three quadrants was being received in the LZ. The A/C take off was completely vertical for 120 feet then movement forward. The gunships placed fire on the flanks of the approach and departing UH-1H helicopters and through their complete disregard of their personal safety these crews made it possible, when no other system could make it possible, to extract the surrounded forces. The extraction was completely successful. All of the live and wounded were extracted although the dead could not be reached because of the intense enemy fire in the area. Not one troop carrying helicopter received any damage through the fantastic team performance of the crews in the seemingly impossible LZ, and through the amazingly close fire support furnished by the gunships who continued to operate at tree top level. As the last lift was completed a company sized force of NVA was seen massing 900 meters to the north of the position in an attempt to overrun the ground forces. Had this lift not been completed it is most probable that the entire friendly ground force would have been destroyed.

The slick crew were AC's WO Borders, WO Benton, 1LT Schmidt, WO Rice, WO Dyer, WO Baker, WO Howard, WO Peters (119th AHC). The Pilots were WO Thybony (119th AHC), WO Fish, 1LT Heslin (119th AHC). 1LT Lindsey, WO Sonier, WO Swint, WO Sparks, WO Brooks. The Crew Chiefs were SP4 Hayes, SP5 Sullivan, SP 4 Miller, SP5 Springberg, SP5 Reimer, SP5 Kock, SP4 Ralph E. McJunkin (119th AHC), SP4 James M. Pyland (119th AHC). The

C&C ship & mission commander was MAJ Sanders, ass't mission commander and pilot MAJ Leva, crew chief SP5 Alden, and gunner SP4 King. Gunner SP4 Desper, SP4 Hebert, SP4 Groves, SP4 Goff, SP5 Karnes, SP4 Cheek, SP4 Charles M. Corbet (119th AHC), Nicholas Postolites (119th AHC).

In view of the extreme danger of the mission, the difficulties presented by the landing zone and the constant hazard of enemy fire I strongly recommend the mission commander and C&C ship AC MAJ Sanders for the Silver Star, the ass't mission commander and C&C pilot MAJ Leva for the DFC, all other AC's for the DFC the remainder of the crew for the Air Medal with "V" device."

(Signed)
John J. Holland
Cpt. Inf.
FOB #2
Hornet Company Commander

CHAPTER **8**

MAYDAY! MAYDAY!

THERE WAS AN area in Laos that had the code name "Hotel 9," which designated a geographical area near an east-west river about 30 km inside Laos and directly west of the tri-border area, where the borders of Laos, Cambodia and South Vietnam intersected. Intelligence indicated that the target area, "Hotel 9," had a large communication center and a transportation node for traffic coming down the trail. It was suspected that there was an underwater bridge that allowed truck traffic to cross the river in that area. At that point the river had two big loops which, from the air, looked like a big bra. The word "bra" was often used as a quick reference for that area.

The mission came down in early December to insert a large force of about 40 men into the area. The force, known as a Hornet Force, was made up of a few American Special Forces personnel, while most of the force consisted of indigenous personnel, most of them Montagnards, indigenous peoples of the Central Highlands of Vietnam. We inserted the Hornet Force on Dec. 10 with heavy air support. I remember being in the lead ship, and as we landed in the LZ, the crew chief reported seeing a large black cable running underneath our aircraft. It was clearly a communications cable for a large enemy unit. That was reported to the SOG Tactical Operations Center (TOC) when we returned to base.

It was not long before the North Vietnamese responded with large-scale attacks against the Hornet Force. Casualties quickly mounted for them and it became evident that they could not survive if they were left in their position. The fighting was fierce and there was a need to bring in water and ammunition. My helicopters were staging out of the Dak To airfield. The airfield was near the Laos border and provided both fuel and ammunition for our aircraft. We could monitor the action on our FM radios as we waited to get the order to launch.

Finally, late in the afternoon of Dec. 11, the order came to resupply the Hornet Force with water and ammunition. My flight of eight UH-1 helicopters and six UH-1C gunships were ready to go. We thought we were going to try to extract the unit, but that was stopped because the fire in the area was too intense. Instead, I would fly in with a single load of water and ammunition, and I would be covered with four of my gunships and some Air Force fighter-bombers. On any SOG mission, our flight package always included at least one empty UH-1 as a chase ship that had the mission of recovering any air crew shot down.

I went out with two chase ships that day. We were running out of daylight, but as I arrived in the area of the LZ, I could see the colored panel marking the LZ, which was nothing more than a small hover hole among a bunch of heavily damaged trees. It was clear that there was not enough room to land, so I would have to come to a hover in the LZ. I did not know how close I could get to the ground. The Air Force bombed the area around the LZ as close as they could, to try to suppress the enemy fire. I decided the only way I could get in was to do a high circling approach. To do that, I came in from about 3,000 feet above the ground and literally put the aircraft out of trim and laid it on its side so it would drop like a rock. I needed to get the highest rate of descent I could get in order to limit the amount of exposure to small-arms fire. In this kind of approach, timing was everything and you had to pull in maximum power at the last minute to stop your descent before you hit the ground. It took a lot of skill to perform this kind of tactical approach.

With my gunships laying down suppressive fire, I made my descent. We received significant fire but the gunships and the ground forces were able to suppress it enough for me to get into the hover hole. We could not get close to the ground because the LZ was on the side of large hill and the damaged trees blocked my descent to the ground. My crew chief and gunner were able to get water containers and ammunition out the door and into the hands of the troops on the ground.

At that point, it would have been impossible to pick up any of the wounded. The LZ had to be improved, or the force would have to move to a more usable LZ.

I came out of the LZ, and as I got above the trees the enemy fire picked up. I made a rapid turn and low-leveled out of the area at treetop level. It was getting dark and we returned to the FOB. All aircraft returned safely, but I believe a couple of the gunships had taken hits.

That night, there was a briefing in the TOC. It was clear the Hornet Force was in deep trouble and at risk of being overrun. They had wounded they needed to get evacuated before they could move to another location with a better LZ.

The mission was set for the next day, Dec. 12. I was the air mission commander and flight lead. I had been into the LZ once and knew the area. The troops on the ground were able to use some of their claymore mines to blow up a couple of the damaged trees to make a little more room for me.

Early on Dec. 12, we staged out of the Dak To

airstrip again. We waited to get the word to launch on the mission. We went in with five lift ships and six gunships. The plan was for me to fly lead into the LZ to pull out the worst of the wounded, followed by another ship to pick up the rest of the wounded. The remaining three lift ships were to fly as chase aircraft, ready to re-cover any crews shot down.

We launched about noon and flew out to the vicinity of the LZ. The troops on the ground had improved the LZ a little. Air Force fighter-bomb-ers had been working over the area all morning, and the troops on the ground reported that en-emy fire was light at that point.

For this mission, I carried a Special Forces medic with me. Sgt. 1st Class Luke Nance, a very ex-perienced medic, was with us that day on my aircraft. He provided a witness statement of the events that followed. I have included that wit-ness statement below. (This statement has been reproduced exactly as the original, signed copy that I have in my files.)

>"On 12 December 1967 while in sup-
>port of a classified mission we received

word that our unit was in heavy contact with an enemy force and had, at the time 12 wounded personnel and 4 KIA. Some of the wounded were in critical condition and required immediate extraction in order to save their lives. A slick piloted by Platoon Leader, CPT John Heslin and Aircraft Commander, WO Brayton Witherell; Crew Chief, SP5 Hartsfield; Gunner, SP4 Mantayne and myself, the medic, was to be the first chopper into the area to extract the seriously wounded. As we arrived at the area and started into the LZ the enemy opened with a barrage of automatic weapons fire, CPT Heslin quickly informed the gunners to return the fire, and unhesitatingly continued the dangerous descent to the LZ, intent only in extracting the wounded. With exceptional flying skill he and the aircraft commander maneuvered the helicopter between trees, high stumps, and unlevel ground. The terrain was so rugged they could not land and hovered 3 to 5 feet off the ground while I was putting the wounded men in the chopper. The aircraft was taking hit after hit from the intense enemy fire. The gunners were furiously laying out effective fire to cover the ship. I put as many of the wounded in the helicopter that it was capable of carrying and again CPT Heslin and WO Witherell began to maneuver the aircraft out of the battle zone. The helicopter receiving multiple hits and finding their mark forced us to crash land in the midst of the enemy unit. The gunners again threw out a wall of machine gun fire killing several of the NVA. One of the gunners, SP5 Hartsfield, expended all of his ammo, and snatched up an M-79 and began showering the NVA with 40mm rounds. CPT Heslin immediately took command of our situation and formed us into a perimeter to defend our position. The chase helicopters, aware of our situation, came in to extract us. Completely disregarding their own safety, CPT Heslin and SP5 Hartsfield left their defensive position and repeatedly exposed themselves, under intense enemy fire, to carry the wounded to the rescue helicopters. WO Witherell and SP4 Mantayne were fighting fiercely, exposing themselves numerous times, to insure the wounded could be loaded and evacuated. After the wounded were secured we then allowed ourselves to be extracted. The personal bravery and precise teamwork of these 4 men in the face of certain disaster is of the highest caliber. Many lives were saved because of the heroism displayed by each of them. I highly recommend that CPT Heslin, WO Witherell, and SP5 Hartsfield be awarded the Silver Star for gallantry in action and that SP4 Mantayne be awarded the Distinguished Flying Cross."

(Signed)
Luke Nance Jr.
SFC E7, RA13627812
FOB #2, APO 96499

When I was picked up by the chase helicopter flown by Warrant Officer Jack Breedlove, I was taken to a radio relay station, located on the very top of a large mountain in Laos known as Leghorn. The site was run by the Special Forces group in support of the SOG mission. Although it had been attacked many times, it had survived because of its location and defenses. It was never overrun during the entire war. I had been into the landing pad at Leghorn a number of times previously to bring in resupplies. It was a very small sandbag LZ perched on the very tip of the mountain. It was difficult to make an approach and land in the LZ because of its location and the high winds that often blew over the site.

After the remaining aircraft had exited the battle area, I was picked up at Leghorn and brought back to our staging area at Dak To. I found out later that when I was shot down, two gunships had been hit hard and one of them went down, as well as an Air Force F4 Phantom that had been flying close air support for the mission. All in all, it was a pretty dark day. Although we got out the worst of the wounded, there were other wounded that needed to come out.

At Dak To, I climbed into one of the other helicopters, and with a new crew headed back out to the LZ to get the rest of the wounded. However, as I approached the area, darkness had set in, as well as bad weather, and the SOG command group decided to call off the mission for the rest of the day.

That evening, back at the FOB, I was part of the planning group that planned the extraction of the entire remaining force for the next day. It was agreed that the unit would make its way through the night to a better LZ about 1 km away. With the help of fire support from Air Force gunships during the night, the unit was able to complete the movement to the alternate LZ.

We launched early the next morning, with me as the air mission commander and lead ship to rescue the entire force. Although we received small-arms fire, we were able to extract the entire remaining force without further damage.

Flying in Vietnam during the war was extremely stressful and intense. A small error often meant life or death for oneself and one's crew. I saw many helicopter wrecks, often with the helicopter ending up in a big orange ball of fire. One of my great fears — and I think it was the same for most of us who flew — was to end up in a ship on fire. I still think of that to this day.

CHAPTER 9

Bombs On The LZ

AS THE AIR mission commander, I took the nightly briefings in the FOB operations bunker. It was clear that the "targets" for our missions were being selected at a very high level. Present at those briefings was usually the FOB commander; his operations officer, or S-3; the team leader that was going to be inserted; and usually the Special Forces FAC, or forward air controller. The FAC had the call sign of "Covey" and he served as a radio relay for the team on the ground and would coordinate the air support for the mission. The FAC could be a junior officer or an enlisted man, usually a sergeant.

On the evening of Dec. 15, the next-day operation was briefed. We were to put in a small team that had a reconnaissance mission directly on the Ho Chi Minh Trail in Laos. We had been running a number of missions into Cambodia, but the action seemed to be moving back up to Laos. At that point, it was evident something big was coming down from the north and the Trail was very busy. We were aware of refueling points along the trail and NVA truck parks.

The tentative LZ for the insertion was identified by map reconnaissance and it was decided that we would use a low-level, high-speed approach to the LZ. It was also decided that we would make several fake approaches to areas en route as a means of deception. The intelligence portion of the briefing made it very clear that the NVA had placed personnel on most open areas that could be used as an LZ, so they would know when we went in. At that time, the NVA had also started to put mines on the open areas that might be used as an LZ. We had experienced that already and had to abort a few missions because of mines.

During the briefing, I requested that the FAC use Air Force assets to put some bombs on the LZ before we went in, to detonate any mines that might be there. I suggested that they could hit several of the fake LZs to confuse the enemy. The officer who was designated to be the FAC for the mission pushed back and said it would just alert the NVA and would not be a good idea. I made the case that they would know we were coming anyway and that the bombs would give the team going in at least a little assurance of no mines on the ground so they could off-load and get into the jungle quickly. The camp commander agreed with me and it was set.

I was lead ship and air mission commander the next day and made the low-level approach with fake insertions along the way. As I approached the final LZ, I had an uneasy feeling that there had not been any bombs dropped. I was right. It went badly. Below is a witness statement. (This statement has been reproduced exactly as the original, signed copy that I have in my files.)

"On 16 Dec 67 I observed heroism in the highest order by CPT John Heslin, 119th Aviation Company.

Deep in the enemy's own territory an insertion was being aborted with 3 helicopter loads already on the ground protecting themselves on the LZ as best they could from a well placed enemy mortar barrage. The team had WIA's from the mortars as well as from mines placed on and around the LZ.

It was under these circumstances that CPT Heslin having returned to the launch site to refuel took off to be again the first ship in so that the WIA's, badly mauled by mines and mortar shrapnel, could be evacuated. Enemy small arms fire drove him off in his first attempt, and realizing that the mortar tubes which were obviously zeroed in on the LZ might still be emplaced, CPT Heslin, over the radio "This is Blue 1, I'm going in again." And again automatic weapons fire drove him off together with an explosion which later proved to be an exploding antipersonnel mine. For the second time CPT Heslin broke around and began his third approach. With determination and courage, which under the circumstances was beyond a pilots call, he set his ship down on the LZ, scooped up the WIA's and pulled pitch. CPT Heslin's behavior during this action not only conformed to the highest traditions of an officer in the US Army but rises beyond duty's call to any man. I therefore recommend CPT Heslin for further recognition by receiving an award commensurate with his demonstrated outstanding flying skill and bravery."

(Signed)
Garrett V. Graves
SGT E5, RA13854603
FOB # 2, APO 96499

On the second approach into the LZ, my skid hit a personnel mine, which damaged the skid and a soldier was blown through the aircraft. I quickly came out of the LZ and went around and made my third approach, this time able to land — even with the damaged skid — to pick up the wounded. Eventually all the members of the small team were evacuated.

CHAPTER **10**

This Aircraft Can't Fly

SOMETIME IN LATE December, when we were getting prepared to put a team out on the Trail in Laos, we got an emergency call from a small unit in Laos that claimed they were being followed by a large NVA unit and needed to be extracted immediately. By declaring a "Tactical Emergency," or "TAC-E," they took priority over other missions. The SOG command group authorized us to attempt to extract the small team as soon as possible.

I organized an extraction mission with three lift ships and two gunships to locate the team and pull them out. I was the air mission commander and the lead ship. The small, six-man team was located deep into Laos, which put us at the edge of our fuel range. If we had problems trying to get them out, fuel would quickly become a problem for us. Many times flying the SOG mission into Laos and Cambodia we were at the limits of our fuel range.

When we located the team, they were on the side of a hill in a small LZ with large trees all around it. I did a high and low reconnaissance of the LZ and was thankful I did not draw fire. It was necessary to do a high circling approach and a vertical descent through the trees. I would not be able to get to the ground because of many blown-off stumps, so I would have to hold the aircraft at a hover with my blades just over the tops of the tree stumps. As I let down into the LZ, I had to put my tail between two very large trees in order to keep the main blades clear of the other trees. It was late in the day and I knew if we did not get them out on the first try we would not be able to come back that day.

As I came to a hover, I was receiving precise directions from my crew chief and door gunner on how much room I had on either side of the ship, especially for the tail rotor. They gave me guidance such as "move the aircraft a foot to the left ... bring the tail two feet right," etc. As we hovered in the LZ, it was necessary for my crew chief to reach down in order to grab the hand of a soldier to pull him up into the ship.

At some point his microphone cord became disconnected, and while he thought I was hearing his directions I heard nothing. My main rotor blades struck one of the large tree stumps and my tail rotor was pushed into one of the trees near it. It all happened in an instant. Miraculously, the blade strike caught the bottom of the blade just behind the main spar on the leading edge — a matter of 2 inches at most. Both blades took the hit about 3 feet in from the tips. I immediately pulled the aircraft up and tried to regain control. The team on the ground disappeared back into the jungle, thinking they were about to see a helicopter tear itself apart in the trees. As I tried to steady the helicopter, my pilot, a new lieutenant who had recently joined our unit, tried to open his door to jump out. After some quick colorful words to him about keeping his ass in his seat, I called the guns to tell them I was damaged and going to come out of the hover hole. The aircraft had a violent one-to-one vibration and we could see the silver pieces of honeycomb from the inside of the blades flying around as the blades flexed. It was difficult to hold my feet on the pedals because of the extreme vibration from the tail rotor. I pulled the aircraft up out of the trees and started to move forward. I could not get more than 40 to 50 knots of speed. My gun lead took a look around the ship and said he did not see any other damage, but pieces of the blades continued to fly out.

I prayed hard and headed for Dak To, a trip of about 50 km. I stayed low to the trees, expecting that at any minute I was going to have to flare the aircraft and put into the trees. It was one of the most tense flights I have had in a helicopter.

As soon as I cleared the security wire at Dak To, I put the helicopter down in a field and shut it down. All of us climbed out, and as the main blades slowed to a stop, we could see the extent of the damage to the main rotors, which was amazing. The tail rotor was also badly damaged and bent.

Not long after that, the unit maintenance officer came up from Pleiku to look at the damage. As he walked around the ship, he just kept shaking his head and saying this helicopter simply could not fly. They ended up getting a chinook helicopter to sling load it back to Camp Holloway for repairs. I got in another helicopter and went back to the FOB to plan the next day's missions.

CHAPTER **11**

Christmas At The Leprosarium

DURING THE TIME I was living at the FOB camp, in late 1967, there was a leprosarium/ hospital run by, I think, a Belgian Catholic nun who had other nuns working with her. The leprosarium was about 10 to 15 km west of Kontum City. From time to time, the SF FOB camp commander would ask me to help the nuns, using one of our helicopters to pick up supplies or even small animals. The camp commander was also very helpful in providing whatever he could to help the nuns.

On Christmas of 1967, the camp commander and I were invited to the leprosarium for dinner. It was amazing. We drove out in a jeep. It was late afternoon, and when we arrived we were brought to a small open patio area where a small table was set up. The nuns waited on us, and just the two of us had a wonderful meal. We asked the sister superior to join us, but she declined, saying this was just for us.

After the dinner, we were taken into a large room and given seats in the middle of the room. In front of us were maybe 20 to 30 beautiful little children — the girls in white dresses and the boys in white shorts. Most of the children were Montagnards. As we sat there, the children sang a series of Christmas songs in English and finished with "Silver Wings Upon Their Chest," which was the Ballad of the Green Beret, a popular song at the time about the SF paratroopers. They sang in near-perfect English. When they finished, we were given two large bags of toys to hand out to the children — the toys had been donated and flown up from Saigon.

It was such an amazing sight. Each of the children came forward, one at a time with the youngest coming first — big, bright smiles on their faces and an English "thank you" when they received their gift.

These were the children of the lepers, who were in the shadows in the back of the room. When the children were finished, they also came forward to thank us — in Vietnamese. You may have seen lepers. The ravages of the disease on their faces was a sight to remember. I will never forget that evening.

When we left the leprosarium, the sister superior insisted on riding in the front seat of the jeep to take us back. It was now dark, and although I had my pistol with me, as did the camp commander, neither of us thought we would have enough firepower if we ran into an ambush on that little dirt road that night. The sister's waving white robe was clear to see, even in the dark as we drove through the night with our lights on. On several occasions we saw VC troops come out of the darkness with their AKs in hand, and then just step back into the darkness.

There were other occasions around that time where we could provide limited support for the nuns, and we did.

The leprosarium was also supported by the Catholic bishop in Kontum City. There was a rather large Catholic church in the city, which had a seminary nearby for young men studying to be priests. I remember flying over it when I departed the Kontum airfield flying out to the west.

I didn't know at the time that one of the young seminarians in that seminary would become part of my life years later. That young man left the seminary and went to the university in Saigon. He escaped from Vietnam in April 1975, along with thousands of other Vietnamese refugees in boats, a journey that, for many, ended in death as their little boats sank on the high seas or pirates robbed and killed them. That young man, after spending time in a refugee camp in Louisiana, was sponsored by a family that lived in the same small Rhode Island town that I was living in. He ended up living in our home for more than two years. I helped that young man get into the electrical engineering program at the University of Rhode Island. He met my wife's youngest sister and married her. They had two wonderful children, and after all these years that young man — no longer so young — and his family are loving members of our family. Nothing happens by accident.

CHAPTER 12

Rice Wine

LIVING AT THE FOB with the SF troops was an experience in and of itself. Because they had many different types of weapons, both foreign and American, I had a chance to fire different guns. They had a small range, and I could check out whatever I wanted and take it to the range. It was an interesting time to explore the world of weapons.

The SF soldiers worked very closely with the Montagnards. Most of the soldiers in the SOG teams were Montagnards. The special relationship between the American SF soldiers and these Montagnards was reflected in the fierce loyalty they showed for one another.

At times, the local tribes would have celebrations

and ceremonies, and they would often include the men from the FOB. On one such occasion, I was included in a celebration at a local village not far from the camp. I attended the event with the FOB camp commander, Maj. Hart, and some of the other staff members. There was supposed to be a ceremonial killing of a water buffalo, but somehow the village chief felt the moon and stars were not right, so he just pulled out a .45-caliber pistol and shot the animal in the head. So much for ceremony.

Later, as the festivities unfolded, there was an area set up with large clay jars in a circle, each with a reed straw protruding from the top. We were all invited to sit down at one of the jars and to drink the rice wine inside. Before I went, Maj. Hart had warned me to go easy on the rice wine because it had a very high alcohol content. I took his advice, so I just sipped a little through the straw. It tasted good and I easily could have consumed a lot of it. Some of the other men did not get the same advice, and it became clear in short order that they had made a big mistake. They started just falling over where they sat after sucking on the wine for a while. I was really glad I was not one of them, but I did enjoy the overall event. We all got little brass bracelets from the chief as a token of friendship. I still have mine.

CHAPTER 13

I Can't Fly Anymore

ONE OF THE absolute rules of being an Army pilot was that you were always a volunteer. By that, I mean no one could ever force you to climb in an aircraft and fly it. You always had the option of saying simply, "I quit!" It did not happen often, but I certainly had heard of cases where that happened.

After that fatal accident in my early days of flight training, a number of student pilots simply quit. I also knew of an extreme case of a pilot taking off his wings and saying he would never fly again. It happened to a friend of mine, and without telling the whole story, I will say that on a mission in Vietnam with the 1st Air Cavalry Division in 1965, my friend, who was a warrant officer, flew back to base in an aircraft in which every member of his crew, along with all the infantry on his helicopter, were either killed or wounded. No one escaped being hit but him. The later story of my friend is amazing but it is not for me to tell here.

One morning at the FOB, as my flight of aircraft for the mission that day were all cranking up, one of my young warrant officers, who had been scheduled as the AC for one of the aircraft, came up to my cockpit window and told me he was quitting. He just could not fly again. It was a tense moment. He knew and I knew I could not order him to climb back into the aircraft and fly the mission.

I told him to go back to where he was staying in the FOB and I would see him later. I went to find another pilot to cover the mission.

Although the replacement pilot wasn't happy, he climbed into the aircraft and we flew the mission that day with all of us returning without incident or damage.

Some of my warrant officer pilots were upset

with me for not forcing the issue and making the pilot fly. I understood how they felt. We all knew that any mission could be our last.

Later that evening, I went looking for the warrant officer who had refused to fly. I found him sitting on the side of his cot smoking a cigarette. His face was red and it appeared he had been crying. As I approached, he stood up. I said sit down, and we both sat there on the edge of his cot. He said his aircraft had taken so many hits in the past few weeks that he was sure he was a "magnet ass," and the next hit would kill him. He was terrified.

It is impossible to get in the head of another human being and truly understand what they are thinking or feeling. Fear was part of our everyday experience flying helicopters in combat. I felt it; most of us did. I always said that fear is your friend but panic would kill you. Fear heightened your senses. It made you sharper as the adrenaline raced through your veins. I knew men who became adrenaline junkies. Just about every day was an adrenaline hit flying helicopters in combat. If a pilot told me he never felt fear, I believed he was either lying to me or to himself, or that he was just delusional. I didn't want to fly with someone like that.

I can recall that on some especially difficult combat assault missions, with enemy fire hitting all around us and bombs blowing up almost beside us, the fear would overwhelm me. I clearly remember my knees shaking so badly I could hardly keep my feet on the anti-torque pedals of the aircraft, and I had to bite my lips to the point of bleeding in order to steady my voice while talking on the radio. At times it required an intense act of will to hold the fear down and not let it push me into a panic.

Fear was normal in that setting. What you could not allow to happen was to cross the extremely thin line between fear and panic — panic killed. Panic would paralyze you and you would be unable to save yourself or anyone else. I saw it happen more than once in combat, and I heard the last radio transmissions from doomed pilots who were in total panic mode.

None of us know for sure how we will react to fear until faced with it. We could only pray that when faced with the moment, we would have the strength to stand in the fire and get through it. I would never make the claim that because I had been courageous in one situation I would always be courageous. The lion today could be the lamb tomorrow. We can only hope that we always will face either moral danger or physical danger with courage.

Talking to the young warrant officer that evening, I suggested that while his fear was real, the decision he was making to not fly again because of that fear would have long-term consequences that he didn't realize. He would always have to live with the fact that he quit, and that would be a ghost that would visit him the rest of his life.

We talked some more, and he told me about his wife back home and the fact that they had a child. I told him I, too, had a wife and two children back home. We discovered that we both came from Rhode Island and had memories of the same places. When I left him, I told him I was scheduling him to fly with me the next day as my pilot. I told him I expected him to show up on the flight line early to help me with the aircraft pre-flight inspection. I told him we would be OK and that we just had to stay focused on what we were doing and not let what was happening around us paralyze us.

At first light, he was at the aircraft with me and we flew the mission together. He was a great pilot and the issue never came up again. No one bothered him about it and no one refused to fly with him. Months later, he went home to his family. I never knew what happened to him after that.

CHAPTER **14**

Brownout

DURING LATE DECEMBER 1967 and early January 1968, it was clear that there was a major NVA buildup taking place in the Highlands and throughout the border areas of South Vietnam. We did not know that in just a short while we would be facing one of the most significant events of the war, the TET Offensive of 1968 on Jan. 30. There was growing concern in the Military Assistance Command, Vietnam (MACV) Headquarters in Saigon, and a lot of urgent requests for more information from the recon teams were coming in daily. The problem was that almost every time we put a team on the ground, it was quickly compromised and attacked, and many times we drew such heavy fire we could not even land to put a team in.

The Ho Chi Minh Trail was extremely hot for us.

At one point, the decision was made to put a Hornet Force in, but instead of using an existing LZ, the Special Forces command group decided that we would use bomb craters from a B-52 Arc Light strike. These Arc Light strikes were usually a flight of three aircraft flying at about 25,000 feet. They would drop strings of 500- and 700-pound bombs that would cover an area about ½ km wide and 1 kilometer long. These strikes were often referred to as "carpet bombing."

Thousands of bombs had been dropped along the Ho Chi Minh Trail in Laos over the course of the war without much effect on the flow of troops and material coming south through the tri-border area and into South Vietnam.

The plan that evolved was to make an insertion immediately after a B-52 strike so we could take advantage of surprise and the destruction of the bombs. We were supposed to be in the air and on long final several miles out when the bombs went in, and we were to select an LZ among the many bomb craters created by the strike. That was the theory.

In the planning stage of the mission, I had serious concerns with the numerous unknowns in following an Arc Light strike that closely. I had seen the effects of these strikes and they were truly awesome.

The mission was given the green light. I was the air mission commander and the lead ship for the assault. As the air mission commander, I had the authority to call off a mission if, in my judgment, it was likely to fail.

The strike was to take place at about 10 in the morning deep in Laos, and I was to be in the air with my lift ships and guns to make the insertion as soon as I could after the bombs had exploded. It was a clear day and it was easy to see the strike going on several miles in front of us. As we approached the target area, there was considerable dust in the air but we could see individual bomb craters.

I selected the best area I could see and started a long descent into a bomb crater LZ. As we got closer, it was clear there were a number of tree stumps and smashed trees all around the craters. The gunships did not have to do a gun run because we were certain there would not be any enemy alive to shoot at us.

I selected my final approach path into what looked like a large crater and started a vertical descent over the tops of the heavily damaged trees. As I got close to the ground to come to a hover in order to let out the troops, the rotor wash from my helicopter immediately picked up clouds of dust, which totally enveloped the aircraft, making it impossible to see. The pilot with me, who had his hands on the flight controls, threw up his hands, shouting, "We are all dead!" I grabbed the controls, looked at the instrument panel for orientation, and pulled the aircraft straight up out of the brown cloud. No one had anticipated the powdered dust from the bombing. While I had made landings in heavy dust, I had always been able to take the aircraft directly to the ground as long as it was a level surface. In this case, it was impossible with the debris and tree stumps everywhere. The only thing we could do was come to a hover, which was impossible to do with the dust hampering our view of the ground.

As soon as I climbed up out of the dust, I called off the mission and we all headed back to base. When we got back, I got considerable push-back from the SOG command group. However, when the FAC returned to base and reported what he had seen, his only comment was he had no idea how we were able to come out of the instant dust storm. We never tried that again.

CHAPTER 15

Hobo Off My Right Wing

ONE OF THE most important missions we could have was to recover the body of a fallen soldier. In Vietnam, the stories were legendary of herculean efforts to recover a soldier's body.

One day, I believe in January, a call came into the FOB tactical operations center that an Air Force FAC (Forward Air Controller) had spotted what looked like a Caucasian body lying naked in a clearing in Laos not far from the border. Our flight had been standing by at the Dak To airstrip on alert to respond to the SOG teams in the field. The order came to launch and make contact with the Air Force FAC on station to see if we could recover the body. As we approached the area, the FAC pilot oriented me on the location of the body and said he was calling in two Air Force A1-E close air support aircraft to give us some cover.

The A1-E was a massive single-engine fighter/bomber that resembled many of the WW II-type fighter aircraft. It was capable of carrying large numbers of bombs and rockets, and had wing-mounted machine guns. Because it was a prop-type aircraft, it could fly a lot slower than the fast-moving jets, and it also was heavily armored to protect it from ground fire. We used to call them "flying tanks." We were always glad to get a flight of A1-Es to support us. They were Douglas Skyraiders. The call sign for the A1-Es was usually "HOBO" or "Sandy," followed by a number that identified which aircraft it was.

On this day, an A1-E aircraft checked in with the FAC, saying he was available to provide support for our mission. I was pleased to have him along.

There had been a few occasions where the NVA had laid out bodies for us to find, which later proved to be a trap. They knew we would come to recover the body, and they would wait to ambush us when we tried to land.

With the help of the FAC, I was able to locate the body on the ground. It appeared to be laid out spread eagle, naked. It appeared to be a Caucasian. I was flying the lead aircraft and started my approach into the small LZ. I had my gunships fly ahead of me to see if they drew fire from the ground. The A1-E reported that he was "on station" above us and ready to cover us if needed. I was on a long final approach. The gunships cleared the area without incident.

Suddenly I started receiving a heavy volume of ground fire from the vicinity of the LZ. I called on the radio that I was receiving heavy fire and would try to break out to my left.

Just then, I looked out to my right side and saw this huge old A1-E with his flaps down, and his landing gear down, so he could fly slowly near me. It looked to me that the enemy fire moved away from me and to concentrate on the A1-E. I was sure he was taking hits for me but he just stayed there.

I broke out to the left and gained altitude as quickly as I could, informing the helicopters behind me to abort the mission. In the distance I could see the A1-E pull up his gear and fly off.

It had been an ambush.

When we got back to the FOB later on, the Special Forces folks did not know of any missing in action that might have been the body. We did not go back again.

I never knew the name of the name A1 - E pilot that day, but I was grateful he was there to help.

For years, the memory of that mission and the details of the A1-E dropping his landing gear and lowering his flaps troubled me in terms of the accuracy of my memory. It seemed incredulous that the A1-E pilot would have done that; yet, I could see it in my memory. I continued doubting myself on that detail until I met a man from Ohio named Ken. When I met him, he recognized that I was a Vietnam veteran by the vest I had on, which had a Vietnam War veteran's patch. He said he, too, was a Vietnam vet and, as is traditional for Vietnam veterans, we said, "Welcome Home Brother!" As we were talking about our mutual experiences in the war, Ken told me he was an electronics system operator in the back seat of a Navy Douglas A1 Skyraider during the war. He said his unit call sign was "Zapper."

I told him my story about the A1-E coming down close to me and slowing down by dropping his landing gear and lowering his flaps. I asked him if he had ever experienced that during his missions in Vietnam. He immediately said yes; they had done that on a number of occasions to slow the aircraft down. He said when they did, the aircraft shuddered and vibrated quite a bit but it was not a problem for them. Once they pulled up their landing gear and their flaps, the aircraft smoothed out and they were fine.

That chance meeting with Ken helped me with that memory. While I am more comfortable now with what I remembered, I still can't be absolutely certain of that detail in my memory. I am comfortable with the rest of the memory.

CHAPTER 16

King Bees

A UNIQUE EXPERIENCE I had while flying the SOG mission was the opportunity to work with Vietnamese Air Force (VNAF) pilots. There was a small group of VNAF pilots who flew old American CH-34 helicopters. In the South Vietnamese military, all the helicopters were Air Force aircraft, not Army.

This small group of CH-34 pilots occasionally worked with the SOG mission. They were called King Bees, and the pilots who flew them had reputations as incredibly brave and excellent pilots. Their aircraft were large and underpowered compared with UH-1 helicopters. Their CH-34 aircraft were old Sikorsky helicopters with a large radial engine. The only armament they had was an air-cooled, .30-caliber machine gun that they would hang in the cargo door for the crew chief to use.

One day, a flight of two King Bees landed at the FOB to support the SOG mission at FOB 2. I remember the names of two of the pilots. One was named "Cowboy" and the other "Mustachio." I believe they were VNAF captains who had thousands of hours of flight time. They were known by all of the SF personnel for their legendary exploits. They were part of the earliest SOG missions flown into Laos in an operation called "Shining Brass." I was told that they received a pretty large bonus for every mission they flew into Laos or Cambodia.

I had a chance to look inside their helicopters and was a bit shocked by what I saw. They all had battle damage to some degree, and I could see large metal cans suspended by coat hangers from the ceiling under the transmission to catch the oil that constantly leaked. The pilots were great guys and offered to take me up for a ride in one of the aircraft. I thanked them, but declined.

They were scheduled to fly with us in a joint

mission to insert a Hornet Force into Laos. At the briefing the night before the operation, we all agreed they would be the last aircraft in the flight and would put their troops into the LZ after we had dropped ours. There was the exchange of call signs and radio frequencies that we would use for the mission. They could speak pretty good English, but it wasn't great.

The next day, early in the morning, we headed out on the mission. I was the air mission commander and flew the lead aircraft. The King Bees were at the end of our trail formation. We had six UH-1s and four gunships followed by the two VNAF CH-34s.

All went well as we approached the designated LZ. The FAC on station reported he had seen considerable enemy activity on the ground in the vicinity of the LZ we planned on using. It was agreed that if we received fire going into the LZ, we would abort the mission and try a different LZ later.

I was the lead ship headed into the LZ with the remaining lift ships following me. Our gunships made a gun run to suppress any enemy fire. It was not long before the gunships reported receiving heavy automatic weapons fire from the ground, and with that information I notified the FAC that I was aborting the mission. The FAC acknowledged my radio call and I pulled out of the approach. Suddenly, from high above me, the two CH-34 King Bees came flying through our formation and went straight into the LZ, firing their machine guns as they went. I could see that they were receiving fire. They never acknowledged that I had aborted the mission. Now we had two loads of troops on the ground in a very hot LZ. Our gunships immediately engaged the enemy on the ground, and our two empty chase ships went into the LZ under fire and pulled out the troops that had been dropped. After they safely got out of the LZ with all the troops aboard, we headed back to base.

When we got back for the debriefing, I explained what had happened with the King Bees and what we had to do to get the troops out. It appeared that there was a failure in communications that could have been disastrous for all of us.

That was the last time I saw the King Bees while I was on the SOG mission. I heard later in my tour that both Cowboy and Mustachio had been killed in action. I don't know if it was true, but they certainly had been testing the odds.

Around the time that the King Bees had arrived, a single American Air Force UH-1 flew into the FOB. I had never seen one of these helicopters before. It, like the others I'd heard of, had a light green and brown camouflage paint scheme and a different engine than our helicopters. The one I saw also had a mini-gun mounted in the door instead of the M-60 machine guns we used.

Their call sign was "Green Hornet," and I found out these helicopters were a dedicated Air Force unit, the 20th Special Operations Squadron in support of the SOG mission. These were UH-1F helicopters. They flew SOG missions farther south, with most of their missions going into Cambodia. I also learned that they operated regularly with the VNAF King Bees. The aircraft and crew did not stay very long and I never saw them again.

For some of the missions we ran in support of SOG, we used specialized equipment. One of those items was called a McGuire rig extraction system, also known as "strings." The McGuire rig was essentially a system of four 100-foot ropes secured to the floor of the helicopter cabin with ropes and 2-by-4 pieces of wood. There were two ropes for each side of the aircraft, giving us the capability to lift four men at a time. At the end of the ropes was a harness-like seat so a soldier could buckle himself in.

The SF personnel installed the system in our aircraft each time we were scheduled to use them. At the anchor point inside the aircraft, a piece of tape was attached to one of the ropes. At the bottom, that same rope also had a piece of tape on it. The plan was that the American soldier in the team would make sure he got into the rig with the tape on it. In the cabin of the aircraft, there was a small hatchet that could be used to cut the ropes if we got in trouble, such as getting hung up in trees. The plan was to only cut the ropes without the tape. I never knew of a time when the ropes had to be cut.

We practiced flying with the McGuire rigs around the vicinity of the FOB. It was difficult to get used to working with them because the ropes extended down 100 feet, so you had to come to a high hover and hold it there. Trying to keep the aircraft steady and holding your altitude was a challenge. The SF personnel offered to let some of the flight crews strap into one of the dangling seats and be flown around, to experience what it was like to be at the end of a "string." Some did; I did not.

When you are at a high hover, you don't have the benefit of ground effect to hold the helicopter up. Ground effect is created by the force of the air being pushed down from the helicopter by the main rotor blades. The air is compressed against the ground and that helps lift the ship. Without it, more power is required to hover the aircraft. In addition, with four men attached to the ropes, you had to fly straight up to be sure you cleared the surrounding trees to avoid dragging the men through the treetops. That was always a great fear with using the "strings."

I can remember a few missions that required us to use the system to extract small teams. Mostly it was in Cambodia. I can only remember flying a helicopter with "strings" one time, which was enough for me. Fortunately it all went well and we didn't get fired at. When hovering high over the trees, you were very vulnerable to enemy ground fire.

During the last week of January, we had 57th AHC pilots and crews join us on the SOG mission. The 57th, which was the unit I originally deployed with, was assigned to Kontum, and the company, along with all the aircraft and maintenance facilities, were locating in tents and bunkers on the north side of the Kontum airfield. The airfield had a concrete runway, long enough to accommodate Air Force aircraft such as the four-engine C-130 cargo airplanes. Many other smaller aircraft routinely landed at the airfield. There was an airport tower operation to control the aircraft and airspace around the field, and a large refueling and rearming area alongside the runway. There was also a number of local Vietnamese militia assigned to the airfield for security.

The 57th was deployed to Kontum specifically to be the AHC in direct support of the SOG mission. With their arrival, there was no longer a need for the other helicopter units, such as the 119th, to rotate through 60-day deployments to the FOB. Most of us were very happy about that because the FOB SOG mission was always high risk, with usually significant combat damage to our helicopters and high rates of crews being wounded and killed.

When the crews came over to join us on the SOG mission, I knew a number of the pilots from the time I was with them at Fort Bragg. Because they were already living at Kontum and operating out of the airfield, they could stay in their own facilities rather than moving in with the Special Forces teams at the FOB. That had both a good and bad side to it. I thought living with the SF team members created a very close bond between the aviation crews and the soldiers we were supporting.

The living conditions for the men of the 57th were difficult, with mud and dirt to contend with nearly all the time, not to mention the occasional enemy mortar rounds fired into their compound. We all had mud and dirt issues, but they had it worse than most.

When they started flying with us, we mixed in their crews with us to orient them on the area of operation (AO) as well as the details of the mission. They all seemed pretty excited about what they were going to be doing. What is it they say? Ignorance is bliss, or something like that.

On Jan. 30, I moved all my men and equipment out of the FOB as the 57th assumed full responsibility for the mission. Flying back to Camp Holloway at Pleiku, I was thankful all of our crews were coming back without losing anyone. Although my aircraft was lost to combat damage, and other aircraft had pretty significant damage, the crews only had minor wounds for the 60-plus days the unit had been on the mission. For me, it was more like 70 days.

The Vietnamese Tet New Year's celebration was about to begin, and there was a lot of talk about a stand-down and temporary cease-fire during the days of celebration. It was the biggest holiday of the Vietnamese year, with families traveling to visit relatives and many of the South Vietnamese Army (ARVN) soldiers taking leave to be with family. No one expected the horror show that was about to explode across the entire country.

CHAPTER 17

TET 1968

IT IS WELL beyond the scope of what I am trying to accomplish here to describe in detail the huge enemy offensive that was launched on the night of Jan. 30, 1968. It was one of the largest campaigns of the entire Vietnam War, with tens of thousands of Viet Cong and North Vietnamese soldiers attacking South Vietnamese, American and allied forces. It lasted for months, costing thousands of lives, both military and civilian, and all of us who were there to experience it will never forget it. In the end, it was a resounding defeat for the communist forces, which suffered enormous losses of men and material. The horrors of death were visible throughout the country, with most of it taking place in the cities and towns.

During that period, we would occasionally get a chance to read a Stars & Stripes newspaper, a military publication offering news about the war, and national news as well. Many of us were shocked to read articles about the Tet Offensive which were not reflective of our experiences at all. The presentations in the newspaper articles, especially the national news, indicated that the Tet Offensive was a disaster for the South Vietnamese and Allied forces. Letters I received from home at that time also told the news of the huge loss, and my family was more concerned than ever for my safety.

While we were well aware of the scope and breadth of the attacks, we could see with our own eyes the devastation of enemy units who were being killed by the thousands. It was, in our view, a victory for us. None of the South Vietnamese military units turned on the government, and hardly any of the civilians were supportive of the communists. What was being said in the news at home was 180 degrees from what we were seeing every day. Because we were a helicopter unit, we had an opportunity to see wide areas of the countryside and had a pretty good look at what was happening. We could not understand how our leaders could be getting it so wrong.

Although it was evident to many of us, especially those of us who had been flying missions on the Ho Chi Minh Trail, that something big was going to happen, the ferocity and breadth of the assaults caught almost everyone by surprise.

In Pleiku, all the installations came under attack. At Camp Holloway, we received many rocket attacks from large 122 mm free flight, Soviet-made rockets. When they hit the ground, they created a hole about 8 to 10 feet in diameter, depending on the ground it landed on, and they could kill anyone within 30 meters of the impact. The rockets had a range of about 8 to 10 miles. When fired, you could hear them coming with a loud screeching sound. Sometimes you could hear the muffled sound of them being launched. Because of the power of these rockets, they were among the most feared weapons the communists used against us in that period of the war. They were often used by small teams of Viet Cong who would set up the rockets and fire them at us before we could react. I have been under 122 mm rocket attack a number of times, and it is a sobering experience.

There were also numerous attacks by mortar fire. We called these "attacks by fire," or ABFs. The 82 mm mortars used by the VC and NVA were similar to our own 81 mm mortars. They were fired from a tube, and most of the time you could hear the round being fired because of their relatively short range. The round would fly high into the air and then arc down to its target. In my opinion, although they did not create the same level of damage that a 122 mm rocket did, the enemy seemed to be much more accurate with the mortars. It was not unusual to see them "walk" their rounds up to our flight line by continually making adjustments with each round fired. They made a very distinctive sound when the round hit and exploded. Throughout my first tour in Vietnam I came under enemy mortar attack many times.

During the Tet Offensive, all of the flight crews would spend the night in defensive trenches and bunkers on the perimeter of the airfield. Because I was a platoon commander, I was responsible for a designated sector to cover against enemy attacks on our perimeter. It was a very stressful time, not knowing if or when the enemy soldiers would try to penetrate our defensive positions. Many times, soldiers on the line would think they saw approaching enemy and would fire massive amounts of rifle — M-16s — and machine gun fire. It was always dicey to get control of the line when that happened. This was night time with a bunch of folks who generally lacked the skills of an infantry soldier.

The enemy often concentrated their rocket and mortar fire on the living areas of the compound. As a result, there was considerable damage to the tent-like structures we called hooches. During one of these attacks, one of our NCOs was killed by a mortar round that hit right beside him. It was a sobering experience for all of us. After every attack, we had to inspect our aircraft for damage and make necessary repairs so we could fly the next day.

During the months of February and March 1968, I spent a lot of time in those often-muddy trenches and then would get out at first light to get ready for a flight mission. Not much sleep for any of us.

There were reports that some parts of the perimeter were probed during that period, and I believe a couple of enemy bodies were reported, but I never saw any of that so I could not be sure they actually were in the wire.

One of the stories that made the rounds was that the Vietnamese barber who had a small barber shop on the compound was actually a communist VC and had been killed in the wire trying to penetrate the perimeter. I can't remember if that was ever confirmed.

Other compounds in the Pleiku area were hit with ground assaults and mortar and rocket attacks. I was told that some of the smaller South Vietnamese positions near the Pleiku airbase were overrun.

During the Tet Offensive, we conducted a lot of missions to air assault units around the area of operation in an attempt to blunt the attacks. There were a lot of medevac missions and resupply missions for units cut off and unable to be resupplied by road. Although it was getting toward the end of the dry season in the Highlands, I remember a good bit of rain and low clouds, which always made flying a challenge.

Because the enemy had infiltrated the cities and towns, we put a lockdown on our personnel from leaving the base. You could not tell who the enemy was, because the VC mostly did not wear a recognizable military uniform. Most of the Vietnamese farmers wore black, loose fitting pants and a black top that looked like pajamas. Often the women dressed the same. You just never knew if someone would suddenly pull out an AK-47 assault rifle and start shooting, or throw a hand grenade at you. Our rules of engagement required us to identify the source of fire coming at us before we could return fire. It was often very difficult to identify exactly where it was coming from or who was shooting at us.

It was hard for us, but it was extremely hard for the Vietnamese civilian population. The brutality of the enemy forces during that period was epic, and the slaughter of innocent civilians was happening throughout the country. While we had our challenges at Camp Holloway and Pleiku, other areas were hit much harder.

The city of Kontum was almost overrun when the Viet Cong, together with a regular NVA regiment, attacked the city and were able to defeat many of the local units making up the regional force. We called these units, similar to our National Guard units, "Ruff Puffs," because they were Regional Forces and Popular Forces. Often they were not well-equipped or led; and because they lived with their families, whenever the fighting got really tough they would sometimes try to leave with their families, creating significant gaps in the defensive positions.

There was, in the city of Kontum, a hospital run by a female doctor from Seattle, Dr. Patricia "Pat" Smith. She had opened her hospital in the Highlands in the 1950s and it was staffed mostly by Europeans and volunteers. In many ways, Dr. Pat was a legend and her work was known far and wide. Her dedication to the local Montagnard people was total. In return, they loved her.

When the communist forces assaulted Kontum during the Tet Offensive, they hit Dr. Pat's hospital hard, doing great damage to the facility and killing a number of the staff. The story at the time, told by a number of witnesses, was that as the

Communist soldiers came running through the hospital looking for her, many of the staff and some of the patients laid on top of Dr. Pat's body to hide and protect her. Many were killed and wounded, and the hospital was severely damaged, but the enemy never found Dr. Pat and she was spared.

These were hard times for the hospital and for Dr. Pat. Later, when relative "peace" returned to the area, donations poured in from all over the world and a new Dr. Pat Smith hospital was built. I was not there to see it built, but I was there in 1972 to see the new hospital once again totally destroyed by communist soldiers in the Easter Offensive of 1972.

Throughout my experience in Vietnam, I saw real problems for the South Vietnamese fighters, whether they were regular Army of the Republic of Vietnam (ARVN) soldiers or the regional force soldiers. They had been fighting a never-ending war. They grew up in war and they never had a chance to leave the war. Their families were always in harm's way. The casualties among the Vietnamese soldiers were often high. They were sometimes not well-led or well-equipped.

Many people compared them negatively against the NVA solders and even the VC. While the NVA soldiers had to worry about being killed on the battlefields of South Vietnam, for the most part they did not have to worry about their families back in North Vietnam. Yes, we bombed North Vietnam, but we made considerable effort not to cause collateral deaths in the civilian population. Although there were exceptions, it was not policy to kill civilians in South Vietnam, even though it was known that some were family members of VC or communist sympathizers. There were incidents of civilian killings by American and South Vietnamese forces, but they were the exception rather than the rule.

I remember on the first night of the offensive, one of the 57th AHC gunships flew into Camp Holloway. The aircraft, a UH-1C gunship, was flown by the gunship platoon commander. As we watched it come in for a landing, it was obvious the pilot was having trouble controlling it because of heavy combat damage. His aircraft was one of only a few that escaped the destruction at the Kontum airfield. The men of the 57th AHC were fighting for their lives that night as the enemy came through their defensive perimeter, blowing up aircraft and bunkers with satchel charges and grenades. A number of the 57th personnel were killed or wounded, and almost all their aircraft sustained battle damage.

Because of the damage sustained by the 57th that first night, they were unable to support the SOG mission. I was sent back to the FOB with my platoon to once again support the mission. Because of the ongoing Tet Offensive, the SOG mission was scaled back, and we were able to support it at times from our base at Camp Holloway, rather than staying at the FOB. There were nights we stayed there, but there were nights we went back to Holloway. When we were at the FOB, we did not have to man the perimeter, but when we were at Holloway we spent every night out in the trenches and bunkers.

CHAPTER 18

We Are Taking Air Bursts

FLYING INTO LAOS and Cambodia was, at that time, the most challenging flying I had ever done. The mountains, the sketchy weather and the intensity of the enemy fire was a lethal combination that claimed the lives of many pilots and crews. It was truly flying on the edge, which tested every aspect of my mind, body and soul.

That said, the most difficult flying of all was a night flight into the mountains of Laos or Cambodia in bad weather. It was nothing short of a nightmare.

I believe it was at the beginning of February 1968 that I was awoken by the duty officer at the FOB at about 1 a.m. My flight records indicate I flew 8.3 hours, of which 2.3 were at night on Feb. 1.

One of the small teams that had been operating up north in Laos in an area called "Dollar Lake" was reporting heavy contact in the mountains and declaring a TAC-E for immediate extraction. I woke up my crews, got dressed, and went to the Camp Operations Center in an underground bunker. The camp commander and his staff were all there debating what could be done. As I came into the room, they were looking at options to try and save the unit. I could hear the radio chatter from the team in the field, which was being relayed through the Leghorn radio relay site in Laos. The weather was bad, with thunderstorms in the mountains.

The camp commander made the decision to launch a rescue effort as soon as we could get airborne. After listening to all the available information, including that they had no casualties and that they had plenty of ammunition left, it was not adding up to me. They also reported that they had not been in direct contact with the enemy for hours.

I told the camp commander I thought it was a suicide mission with a high possibility of failure, given the location and the weather. I asked if he would consider a first-light launch instead of the night launch. He was not happy with me, and he put a call in to my company commander, Maj. Joe Campbell, back at Camp Holloway. In the meantime, I got my crews up and ready. We would take four lift ships and two gunships.

Maj. Campbell supported the camp commander for the mission, so I launched at close to 2 a.m. Once airborne, I was able to get Maj. Campbell on my radio and told him I thought that this was a suicide mission that was not needed, and we would have a much better chance for success in the daylight. He insisted we try. I told him I was sorry he did not support my judgment and that I was truly pissed off at him.

We headed west at about 5,000 feet above ground level, which kept us above the local mountains. The weather was stormy and we had trouble staying in formation. I was told we would have an Air Force C-130 overhead to drop flares for us when we arrived in the vicinity of the team. I was not happy, but I did not let my crew know how unhappy I was.

All the crews were anxious and highly stressed as we flew out to the mountains of Laos. Along the way, as we approached the border of South Vietnam and Laos, there were flashes in the sky all around us. One of the pilots in the formation cried out on the radio that he was receiving air bursts around his helicopter. I assured him that he was not getting air bursts from enemy anti-aircraft fire, he was seeing the lightning that was all around us.

When we finally arrived, above the clouds and over the team's location, I got a situation report from the team leader. We were able to locate them by homing in on their FM radio frequency. The team leader was a young, very excited SF sergeant. He said he was in a small LZ on the side of a mountain. He said he was not in contact with the enemy and he thought he could see the clouds about 300 feet above his position. At that time the Air Force C-130 pilot came up on the radio to give his location.

The plan was that the C-130 would drop illumination flares through the clouds and the team leader on the ground would give us information on how high the clouds were when the flares broke through. He would also give us a vector from the descending flares to his position.

I told the flight of aircraft to stay high in a wide circle, and that I did not want the gunships to engage unless I had a target for them. When the flares came down, I started a circling descent around the flares, hoping to break out of the clouds before I hit the trees. I had my landing light and spotlight on, which did not help in the clouds but would be critical as soon as we broke out.

On my first attempt I got a bad case of vertigo. I had already instructed my pilot to stay on the instruments, and if I lost it with vertigo I would pass the controls to him so he could fly us back up through the clouds. He did that. On the second attempt, the same thing happened and we came back out again. The team leader on the ground said he had seen my landing light through the clouds and that I was coming down close to his location.

On the third attempt, we broke out of the clouds over the trees and were able to locate the LZ quickly. It was large enough for me to go directly into it and flat enough for me to get close to the ground so the SF team could all jump in. We did not hear or see any enemy fire.

Once I had them all on board, I went back up through the clouds and formed up the flight for the trip back to base. The C-130 pilot checked out of the radio net and headed for home, which I believe was in Thailand.

As we were flying a southeasterly heading back to base, I was hoping the weather would not close down on us. I was wrong. We started getting into thicker and thicker clouds. I had the entire flight tighten up in formation with our external navigation lights on bright so we could see each other. The last thing I wanted was helicopters lost out in the clouds. Many of the pilots struggled with their flight instruments because the only training any of us had with instrument flight was a tactical instrument card, which was the bare minimum if you found yourself in the clouds.

It was about 3:30 and everyone was getting low on fuel. Our helicopter fuel gauges measured the amount of fuel in pounds, rather than gallons. It was an extremely dark night and we kept flying in and out of clouds. I was praying that we were on the correct heading. In those days, we had very limited navigation aids in Vietnam, with most of our flying being dead reckoning off a compass heading.

The flight seemed endless and I wasn't sure if we would have enough fuel to get back. There was absolutely nowhere in that jungle to put it down if we ran out of fuel.

The first fuel call I got was from one of the gunships. The pilot reported his 20-minute fuel light had just come on. The light was an emergency warning to let you know, if it was accurate, that your engine would quit in 20 minutes. It wasn't long before the other pilots reported their 20-minute lights were on, and not long after that, mine came on.

I did not know how far we had to go, or even where we were at that point. I just kept praying. Suddenly I had an idea. I knew that there was a 155 artillery battery located at Dak To, and they were not far from the fuel point. I searched my frequency book for the unit's radio frequency and call sign. I found it and started calling the unit, praying someone would be awake on the radio. After two or three tries, I got a response from their operations center.

I requested that they fire illumination rounds over the top of the Dak To fuel point to guide us in. It was not long before I heard them call the mission as "shot fired," with a delay and then "splash," which meant the round was out and illuminating.

I strained looking through the clouds but saw nothing. Another "shot fired … splash." Off in the distance I could see a very faint glow. Another "shot fired … splash." Yes, there it was off our nose! All the crews saw it. As we headed for the light, I just kept praying that no one flamed out. We all landed at the fuel point safely with very little fuel left in the tanks.

I thanked the Arty guys for their help. I did not know who they were and never found out. We topped off on fuel and safely flew back to the FOB.

CHAPTER 19

First Cobra Flight

BECAUSE THE 57ᵀᴴ AHC was slowly coming back up to full strength after the damage received during the Tet Offensive, we continued to be tasked with supporting the SOG mission at the FOB. It was a bit of a chaotic time for me. We felt stretched as a unit trying to support a wide range of missions. As the weather started to deteriorate in the early spring, it only added to the challenges of flying.

In early 1968 about the time of the Tet Offensive, the Army deployed a new kind of gunship to Vietnam. We had UH-1C model gunships, which had a crew of four men: two pilots and two door gunners. These aircraft would fly alongside us when we were making combat assaults, firing their rockets and machine guns to suppress enemy fire or killing the enemy troops when they found them. The relationship between the UH-1 lift pilots and the gunship pilots was very close. Many times the gunship platoon would recruit "slick" pilots to come and fly with them.

The new gunships coming into country were much different. They were AH-1G Cobra helicopters, often called "Snakes." These aircraft were designed specifically as a gun platform, unlike the UH-1C gunships, which were basically converted lift ships. The new Cobras only had two pilots in them with no door gunners. The aircraft were faster and more powerful than the old "C" model guns. In addition, they used different tactics because of the type of armament they carried and the fact that they did not have gunners hanging out of the doors.

There was a lot of discussion among us at the time on the relative merits of the two types of gunships, but it was clear we would have no choice; the new Cobras would soon replace the entire "C" model fleet.

One day when I was at the FOB, two of the new

Cobras arrived. They were flown by pilots from the 361st Aerial Weapons Company (AWC) with a call sign of "Pink Panther." The two ships that arrived were there to get an orientation on the SOG mission because their company, the 361st, was designated for operational support of the SOG mission exclusively. I was surprised to see that level of commitment by Army leadership to the SOG mission.

That day, I met the crews from the 361st and they let us climb into their new Cobras. Since I remained the air mission commander, one of the Cobra pilots asked if I would like to go up for a brief flight around the area. I was delighted and immediately climbed into the front seat of his helicopter.

In the Cobra gunships, the two pilots sat one behind the other, with the aircraft commander sitting in the back seat and the other pilot sitting in the front seat as the gunner. The front-seat pilot did not have the usual controls of a UH-1 helicopter, but rather had two small controls, almost like joysticks on either side of his seat. In the center was a large movable device used to control and fire the turret guns located underneath the front seat pilot. The turret had a minigun rotating machine gun capable of firing thousands of rounds per minute. Beside that was a 40 mm automatic grenade launcher capable of firing several hundred rounds in a matter of minutes. The aircraft commander in the back seat controlled the 2.75-inch rockets on the wing pods.

These aircraft were state-of-the-art in their day and very effective in their attack and support mission.

On this day, I sat in the front seat as the young captain behind me brought the helicopter up to a hover and then smoothly took off with what seemed to me more speed and power than I was used to in a helicopter. We flew out to the west of the FOB at several thousand feet as the AC oriented me on the capabilities of the aircraft. While we were airborne, we received a call on the radio from a desperate SOG team that was in danger of being overrun just over the border in Cambodia. With this aircraft we could be there in a very short time because it could fly much faster than our Hueys. The ground unit declared a TAC-E, which meant anyone in a position to render assistance was obliged to go to their rescue.

The ground unit commander was requesting immediate fire support to destroy the enemy attacking him, which would allow them to break contact with the enemy and get away.

After a quick radio call back to the FOB, we were cleared to provide whatever assistance we could. Usually Cobras worked as a minimum team of two aircraft, but on that day there was no time to wait for another aircraft to show up.

As we flew to the location of the unit on the ground, the AC oriented me on the use of the gunner's weapons controls. Talk about a crash course on how to shoot a very sophisticated turret-based weapons system. My role as the gunner would be to engage the enemy with the turret weapons as we attacked the position, while the AC fired rockets at the enemy. After the rockets were fired and we turned away from the enemy, I was to use the turret weapons to continue firing at the enemy position to suppress the enemy fire, as we were in a vulnerable position when turning.

As we approached the unit and got our final instructions from the ground unit leader, we started our gun run. We were told, by a very excited man on the ground, that he had a small marker panel on the ground to orient us. He said he was 20 meters north of the panel and he was getting fire from the enemy 100 to 150 meters south of the panel. All I could do is hope he had his directions correct.

On the first pass, the AC fired his rockets at the point indicated by the ground commander and I engaged that point with the minigun, followed by the grenade launcher. As we broke away, I continued to fire the weapons system at the enemy position. Finally we heard the ground unit commander on the radio, elatedly telling us that we were right on target and were having a devastating impact on the enemy. I was so relieved to hear his voice. The AC brought us around for another run, followed by a third attack. After that, the ground commander said the enemy was backing off and he was getting out of the area as quickly as he could. He gave us a quick thanks and then the radio went silent.

We went back to the FOB and landed. It was an experience I never forgot. It was not until I was an Air Cavalry Troop Commander in 1978 with 10 of my own Cobras in the ¾ Cavalry assigned to the 25th Infantry Division in Hawaii that I ever climbed into the front seat of a Cobra again.

Jack Heslin, age six, sitting on the lap of his father.

Jack Heslin in ROTC uniform with his father in the middle and his brother, Joe.

*Jack and Jean Heslin on their wedding day
June 5th 1965.*

Jack Heslin holding his oldest son John at Ft. Wolters TX.

Jack Heslin sitting in the cockpit of a Huey Helicopter.

*In the Huey L-R Dan Baker, Dave Raymond and,
standing at right, Jack.*

Jack Heslin standing beside a Huey gunship.

Jack with his helicopter tail # 66-16516 at FOB2. Three days after this picture was taken Jack was shot down on the Ho Chi Minh Trail and this helicopter was destroyed.

Jack Heslin at FOB 2 with a pet monkey.

*This is an aerial look at the Dak To airfield
looking from south to north.*

On the left is Maj. Hart, FOB 2 Commander, Jack Heslin in the center, unknown SF soldier on the right. The picture was taken at a Montagnard ceremony.

Jack Heslin as the 119th AHC Operations Officer "Gator 3".

Jack Heslin receiving the Silver Star August 1968.

*Memorial at Camp Holloway listing
crew members that were KIA.*

CHAPTER **20**

Pilot Error

ALL OF US who flew in Vietnam fully understood the concept of "pilot error." It appeared that it was pilot error that killed my instructor pilot and fellow student that day at Fort Wolters, Texas. Without a doubt, pilot error was the cause of many deaths in Vietnam. There was not one of us who could honestly say we never made a mistake that could have become a fatal mistake in an instant.

We learned early that to survive flying, you had to "stay ahead" of the helicopter. That meant you had to always be looking to see what was ahead and preparing for the worst. I never flew a single flight where I was not continually looking at the ground for a place to "put it down" if I lost the engine. The key was total, in the moment, awareness of what was happening. It was easy to get distracted by the chaos surrounding you and just lose the bubble of what you were doing in the moment. The noise from the machine with the blades beating the air, the howl of the engine and transmission could be deafening, not to mention constant radio calls in your ears. Add to that the ubiquitous sounds of a combat environment with explosions and gunfire that created a cacophony of mind-numbing noise.

I always felt that if I died of a combat injury or the people in my aircraft suffered combat wounds, there was nothing I could really do about that. It was a level of fatalism based on a strong personal faith that got me through some horrific situations.

On the other hand, if because of an error on my part, a mistake I made, others suffered or I became injured, that would be extremely hard to live with. The daily stress is hard to imagine if you have never been there. Mistakes were made, people died, and sometimes the person responsible had to live with that knowledge for the rest of his life. I am so thankful that it did not happen to me, but it could have — in an instant — many times.

Flying a machine like a helicopter is a unique human experience, and like most man-operated machines, with time and experience flying the machine seemed to become part of one's very being. I am sure many have experienced that feeling with other machines, such as race car drivers on the track or motorcycle riders who have had years in the saddle, so to speak. You can't really describe it, but you know it when you have it. Once you reach a certain level of proficiency, there is a danger that you will start to believe you have "mastered" the machine. When that happens, you are setting yourself up for disaster.

Strapping on a helicopter in a combat situation gets the adrenaline running fast. I believe all pilots get to a point where they think they are pretty good with the machine and they feel like they can handle almost any situation they find themselves in. That's normal. If you did not have enormous confidence in your ability as a pilot, you simply could not climb into the machine and start it up. It is overconfidence that can lead to a tragic error. It can happen in an instant, with no way to recover.

One day I was on a mission from Pleiku to Kontum in a UH-1 helicopter to deliver some troops to a unit at the airfield. They were a bunch of young soldiers who climbed into the back of my helicopter with full confidence that my skill would safely deliver them to their unit. I certainly believed their confidence in me was well-founded.

As we took off that day, there were reports of enemy activity along the route we would be flying to Kontum and it was suggested that we fly at a low level, just at the tops of the trees, to avoid enemy ground fire. That was fine with me, and besides, flying low to the ground added a level of intensity and excitement that you did not experience if you were thousands of feet up in the air.

So off we went, and I was flying as the AC. We followed the major road from Pleiku to Kontum, called QL 14. It was a two-lane highway that cut through the jungle with a few bridges along the way. It was the major resupply route for military convoys between the two cities.

That day I decided I would get "down on the road" so I would be really low-level. I was flying the Huey at about 110 mph down the middle of the road, so low that the helicopter skids were barely off the pavement. At one point the road climbed a hill, and then it was just a cut-through between two large hill masses on either side. There was plenty of room for my rotor blades to fit through the cut, so I stayed on the road going up the hill. Just as we crested the hill, I was face-to-face with an oncoming large Army dump truck.

The Huey had chin bubbles, which were plastic windows just past the pilot's feet, which allowed the pilot to see the ground beneath the helicopter.

It all happened in an instant. I instinctively pulled up on the controls to climb, and in what seemed like an eternity I could see the wide-eyed driver of the truck as we barely cleared his windshield. The abrupt maneuver was perceived by the passengers as a bit of a thrill, which brought smiles to their faces. I knew — and my crew knew — we had just avoided a catastrophic accident by seconds and inches.

When I got up to about 3,000 feet above the ground, I turned the controls over to my pilot in the right seat. All I could do was thank God I had not hit the truck. It was an intense and extremely sobering experience I will never forget. I never "hot dogged" an aircraft again, unless it was absolutely required by the combat situation.

CHAPTER **21**

R & R

DURING THE VIETNAM War, there was a policy in place that provided opportunities for service members, in-country, to be granted an R&R, or Rest & Recuperation, leave after they had completed at least one month of in-country service. The list of destinations included: Hawaii; Sydney, Australia; Bangkok, Thailand; Hong Kong; Kuala Lumpur, Malaysia; Manila, Philippines; Singapore; Taipei, Taiwan; and Tokyo, Japan. Service members going to Hawaii or Sydney were authorized seven days. All other destinations were five days. This allowed for the extra travel time associated with Hawaii and Sydney.

The most popular place for married men to go was Hawaii, because it was the cheapest and easiest place for the wives to go. For single men, Bangkok seemed to be the most popular, because it was cheap and the culture provided female companionship, well-controlled by the government, with required health checks for the women and usually a signed legal document outlining her responsibilities to the client, to include prostitution and transportation.

There were also in-country opportunities for a short R&R. The most popular place was Vung Tau, in the southern coastal area of South Vietnam.

Once you had 30 days in-country, you could put your name on a list for an R&R destination. You did not have much control of exactly when you would get it, but you did get enough warning so you could contact your wife to make travel arrangements. The destinations were basically as space was available.

The rules were very specific about what you could wear and bring with you. If you were going to Hawaii, you usually wore your khaki uniform and you could not take any of your military equipment with you. You would turn in your personal weapons to the unit arms room and leave the remainder of your equipment in a unit storage area, or, if you had a relatively permanent space, such as a hooch or tent space, you could leave it there.

Once you were notified by the Command that your R&R was approved, a set of orders would be cut and sent to your unit authorizing your travel. The unit commander did not have the authority to keep you from R&R, and sometimes extraordinary efforts were made to ensure a soldier got to his departure flight on time. I can remember any number of times picking up soldiers from a field location even while heavy combat was taking place, and flying him back to Pleiku so he could catch a flight to Saigon for his flight out to his R&R destination. Every effort was made to ensure the soldiers got their R&R, whether officer or enlisted.

When you got to your R&R location, you had to change into civilian clothes. Many of us who met our wives in Hawaii had our wives bring some of our civilian clothes in their suitcase.

Most R&R flights out of Vietnam were civilian

aircraft chartered by the military. It was like being on any civilian airline flying in the United States.

When you arrived at your destination, you would be put on a bus and taken to whatever facility you were staying at. Usually there was a gathering area where you would receive a military briefing on the do's and don'ts of your time on R&R, with special emphasis on the absolute need to make your departure time for the return to Vietnam. For those of us who went to Hawaii, the wives could meet us when we got to the gathering area. It was a very emotional time.

One of the saddest things that happened — and it happened when I went to Hawaii — was a young wife waiting to meet her husband, only to be told that he had died in action. They were not able to notify her before she left home.

I had put in for R&R in Hawaii and hoped I would be able to go at about my mid-tour point. My wife was pregnant with our third child at the time, and the last month of the pregnancy that the doctor would allow her to fly was the seventh month. For us, that was March. We had two

children that Jean would have to make arrangements for while she was gone.

As it turned out, my orders came down for the
second week of March, and I was able to meet
Jean in Hawaii for about five days. It was an
emotion-packed time for the two of us. I was trying to decompress, and she was filled with stories about the children and family. Her life, like
those of most wives of men serving in Vietnam,
was challenging. She was living in an apartment
not far from her parents, trying to deal with two
little children and being pregnant with the third.

While it was difficult for us "fighting the war,"
it was also very difficult for the wives who had
to do it all, with no promise that their husbands
would come home safely. It was traumatic at
times.

Jean told me the story of a military sedan pulling
up in front of the apartment and two uniformed
soldiers coming to the front door. She had two
little children hanging on to her as she opened
the door, waiting for what she fully expected to
be the notification of my death in action. She
said she was ready to pass out as she opened

the door to greet the two men. The men asked if she was Mrs. Heslin. All she could do was nod her head yes. The men saw that she was greatly distraught, and said that they had come because we had filed a claim for furniture damage, and they were there to inspect the damage. She broke down and said her husband was in Vietnam, and the two NCOs immediately understood. They helped her to a chair and were full of apologies. They said they didn't know. It was a moment that has stayed with my wife to this day.

Jean and I had a wonderful time in Hawaii, but it seemed like minutes rather than days. Saying goodbye to her at the airport was heart-wrenching for both of us. She was due to give birth to our third child on May 21, and the unspoken thought was, "Will our new child ever know me?"

Hard times ... hard times never forgotten.

When I returned to Vietnam and got back to my unit, I immediately took off my khaki uniform and put on my jungle fatigues and flight gear to resume my day-to-day flight duties. The war continued.

CHAPTER 22

"Light Blue"

MY COMPANY COMMANDER, Maj. Joe Campbell, wanted me to stay as the platoon commander of the Blue Platoon, but the company operations officer, Capt. Roy Ellington, was getting ready to leave to go back to the States. Because Capt. Ellington was close to leaving, he did not want to fly in the AO anymore, so it was rare to hear his voice on the radio. We called him "Duke" Ellington; often we just said, "Here comes the 'Duke'." His call sign as the 119th Operations Officer was "Gator 3."

He was a senior captain with considerable Vietnam experience. In his role as the company operations officer, he coordinated with the various units that we supported every day to ensure we were providing the aviation support needed. The units we supported would provide a "task" sheet every day for the next day's requirements. Capt. Ellington would then assign those tasks to the appropriate platoons, be they the lift platoons or the gun platoon. Each evening, the platoon commanders would check the number of helicopters and crews available for the next day and then assign crews to each mission.

Some of the missions were less stressful than others. We often called such administrative type missions "Ash & Trash," because they generally did not involve a combat assault mission and they were usually from a secure base to a secure base, like airfield to airfield, rather than out in the bush at an LZ. As a platoon commander, I would try to spread the distribution of this type of mission around, so that each of the crews had some opportunities to fly these less stressful missions. If we had a crew member getting close to his DEROS — time to leave country and go home — we would try to keep him off the direct combat assault missions, if possible. It was always a very tense time for those who had been keeping their "short-timer calendar" when there were fewer than 10 days left for them in country.

Most of us kept a calendar in which we would cross out each day, so we could track how many days we had left to DEROS. All kinds of superstitions developed around the "short-timer calendar" as the light at the end of the tunnel started to become clear. Fate had a fickle finger, and there were many very sad stories of men within a day or two of their DEROS being killed on a mission.

None of us felt certain that we were going home until the "big iron bird" lifted off the runway at the Tan Son Nhut Air Base, down near Saigon, with us in it. Most of the time when these aircraft departed, there was a big cheer when the plane lifted off. In most cases, the aircraft were commercial airplanes under contract by the military. They had stewardesses on board, with food and drinks for all. You just can't imagine the feeling of being in one of those beautiful air-conditioned planes as it lifted off the runway and you were on your way home.

Whenever we received taskers from units that

wanted us to conduct a large lift of soldiers into an LZ, it required a lot of coordination and planning. It was the job of the operations officer to pull that planning effort together. A combat assault, also known simply as a CA, could include as many as 20 or more lift helicopters, which may have come from different units, and a CA might also require six to eight gunships, which also may have been pulled from different units.

Usually a CA that involved lifting an American infantry battalion would be scheduled for early in the morning, and last most of the day. If it went badly, with heavy enemy contact, it could last well into the night. Whenever there was a CA, there would be a command & control aircraft flying over the action, directing and coordinating the complex elements that needed to be in place. Artillery support had to be coordinated, as well as Air Force bombers and forward air controllers. Careful planning needed to be done to ensure adequate fuel for the helicopters as well as ammunition for the various weapons systems.

Throughout the operation, communication

between all aircraft, ground units and Air Force support had to be maintained, with everyone knowing what radio frequencies were to be used on each of the radios. It was like a large theatrical production that had many moving parts, all of which had to work with perfect timing if the CA was going to be a success. Needless to say, when the enemy entered into the picture with heavy ground fire, the entire operation just got more complicated.

For the uninitiated, trying to pull one of these operations together seemed overwhelming. It was, at times, very difficult to keep it all straight in one's head, even with a good plan in place.

During my year in Vietnam, I became very familiar with conducting CAs and, as an air mission commander, flying the C&C helicopter with the ground unit commander on board, usually an Army lieutenant colonel battalion commander with part of his staff. It could get very stressful. It was always a matter of life-or-death decisions that had to be made at the moment under great stress.

In early April 1968, the battles around Dak To

continued to rage in the mountains and valleys near the Laotian border.

One day, when I was flying a resupply mission for a 4th Infantry Division battalion south of Dak To, I heard a radio call that an emergency CA was being organized to lift a battalion into a suspected enemy location near the Laos boarder. I checked in with the unit that was making preparations and staging at the Dak To airstrip to be lifted in for the assault. At the time, I was the lift platoon commander, Blue One, and I knew our unit would be playing a major role in the CA. Just as I was the "Turtle" to replace the unit Operations Officer "Duke" Ellington, I had a 1st Lieutenant in my platoon that was my "Turtle." Johnny Shelton, who had a call sign of "Light Blue," was at the airfield ahead of me, organizing the lift and planning to be the lead helicopter into the LZ. After listening to the intelligence reports on the area we were going into, it was clear to me that this could go bad quickly. As the platoon commander, I said I would fly the lead lift ship.

When all the details for the operation were in place to include artillery, gunships and Air Force close air support, we lifted off the runway at about noon. When we arrived at the intended LZ, I could see it was a one-ship LZ, and since my platoon was strung out behind me, each of us would land one ship at a time. I started my approach, closely following behind the last artillery round and escorted by the gunships that were firing into the LZ and the area around it to suppress any enemy fire.

As I flared my aircraft to set it down, I was surprised by how clear the ground was, like someone had deliberately cleared away the undergrowth. I also noticed that there appeared to be well-camouflaged bunkers on either side of the clearing. It was very quiet, with no enemy fire at all. I had a bad feeling. After we unloaded the infantry troops from my aircraft, I took off, followed closely by Johnny Shelton — "Light Blue" — coming in to land behind me. As soon as he put his skids on the ground, the enemy opened a ferocious barrage of automatic weapons fire that immediately killed Johnny's helicopter engine and wounded a number of the American troops on the ground. Johnny put out a "May Day" call, and as I turned to look back,

I could see bursting mortar rounds around his ship. I turned back into the LZ immediately, intent on rescuing Johnny and his crew. Suddenly over the radio I heard this booming voice, "Blue One, get the F—K out of the area now! Now!" It was the "Duke," who had been flying the C & C ship above us and could see everything as it was unfolding.

I was furious with him and said I was going in, and again he told me with very colorful language to get out of the area. He said when we were ready we would go back, but now I would be just another casualty to deal with. I followed his order and we flew back to the Dak To airfield.

When I landed, "Duke" was already there, talking on the radio with the Air Force FAC, desperately trying to get any fighter-bombers he could get a hold of to deliver fire on the enemy positions. Our gunships stayed on station, firing all the ordnance they had at the enemy until they were out of ammunition. They returned to Dak To to refuel and rearm. "Duke" was contacting every gunship in the area that he could reach by radio to bring them to help us.

It took about an hour to get it all together so we could go back out to the downed crew. I was flying lead again with a heavy gunship escort. In the meantime, Johnny and his crew were fighting alongside the infantry troops as they fought their way out of the LZ and were able to move down the mountainside to another small LZ. They were able to take all the wounded with them. It was an incredible relief to me to see "Light Blue" and his crew jump into my ship, along with several infantry troops. I pulled pitch and got out of the LZ as fast as I could. Ships behind me were able to get the remaining soldiers out, and we all returned safely to Dak To. The CA that we started was canceled. It turned out we had landed directly on top of an NVA regimental command bunker.

The "Duke" had probably saved my life. There was never anything said about the exchange of words we had that day. A few days later, Roy "Duke" Ellington packed up his stuff and went home. I became the new operations officer, "Gator 3."

Johnny Shelton and his entire crew were awarded Silver Stars for their actions that day.

On April 24, 1968, Maj. Joseph R. Campbell III, Infantry, changed command of the 119th Assault Helicopter Company, and Maj. Warren R. Porter, Corps of Engineers, assumed command of the 119th Assault Helicopter Company.

Maj. Campbell was a great company commander and I learned a lot from him. He never held a grudge against me for sounding off at him that night when we had to fly the SOG mission into Laos. A smaller man could have made my life miserable for what I said. He could have ruined my military career. He was a professional and understood the pressure I was under that night and it never came up again.

When there is a change of command, the event often triggers a series of administrative actions. One of those is the requirement to write an Officer Efficiency Report (OER) on any subordinate for whom you had direct supervision. In this case, Joe had to write an OER on his direct reports, which included me as a platoon commander. Since the report summarizes Maj. Campbell's evaluation of me, I have included a copy of the narrative portion he wrote on the OER. There were other areas of the report which involved a numerical score that had to be supported by the narrative.

OER written by Joseph R. Campbell III, MAJ, INF 119th AHC Company Commander — 24 April 1968. (This statement has been reproduced exactly as the original, signed copy that I have in my files.)

"Captain Heslin has performed all duties assigned in an outstanding manner. His performance of duty in a combat environment, often times under intense enemy fire was so outstanding that on numerous occasions he was cited for bravery. This in itself is commendable but in each instance he was in a position of great responsibility as either the air mission commander or the flight leader of a battalion sized airmobile operation. He has demonstrated a maturity and judgement, under intense mental and physical pressure, which is seldom found in an officer of his relative youth and inexperience. As a platoon leader he continually displayed a quality of leadership and professional knowledge that is destined to carry him to positions of great responsibility in the United States Army. Not satisfied with the formidable responsibility of platoon leader he constantly sought greater responsibility. His spare time was spent in improving his professional knowledge and he quickly demonstrated his ability to lead the unit in any assigned mission. Captain Heslin has the complete confidence of superior officers and thrives in any kind of challenging situation. Because of his unique and certainly outstanding qualifications he was selected to assume the duties of operations officer for the unit, a position normally filled by the senior officer in the company. For a period of time he functioned not only as platoon leader but the operations officer as well. It is noteworthy that during this time both assignments were carried out in an outstanding manner. I consider this officer's potential to be unlimited and would seek him out to work with me on any future assignment."

Over the years I have had occasional contact with Joe Campbell, who lives in Florida. Our contacts have always been by e-mail. We are all "running out of runway," so I don't know how much longer we will be able to communicate. After all these years, he has continued to be gracious in his comments about me and his appreciation for the job I did while working for him.

A change of command always brought with it stress for all involved, with the known commander leaving and the unknown commander coming in. In a combat unit that stress could be palpable. The Army policy during the Vietnam War was that most command positions were held for only a six-month period unless injury or death shortened that period. On occasion, a truly incompetent commander could be relieved of his command before the six months was up, but I was not aware of that happening very often.

Maj. Warren "Randy" Porter would remain my company commander for the remainder of my tour, which ended on Oct. 11, 1968.

Maj. Porter was an Army engineer and a pilot. When he arrived, I had an immediate rapport with him. I was the unit operations officer, "Gator 3," and in that role I was a key staff officer for the new commander. I was a seasoned combat veteran at that point, and although I was only 24 years old in April 1968, I felt like I was an old man who had already lived several lifetimes. I can't even begin to explain that feeling. I knew I was much older than my years.

The rainy season seemed to be coming on early that year, and the low clouds and heavy rain made flight operations difficult and more dangerous than usual. In the Highlands of Vietnam, the rainy season, which was also known as the monsoon season, slowed the pace of combat activity for both sides. The enemy units struggled with the mud as much as the ARVN and American troops. Most of the time it was a period of consolidation and regrouping and refitting in preparation for the dry season, which would come in September and October. Combat operations certainly did not stop, but there was a noticeable drop-off in the number of missions we flew. The weather slowed everything down.

CHAPTER **23**

"Will I Ever Learn How To Do That?"

SHORTLY AFTER MAJ. Porter arrived, we received a tasker to organize a CA that would involve lifting a battalion of infantry from the Kontum airfield and putting them into two different LZ locations 25 to 30 km west, near the base of a large ridgeline that ran north and south. Maj. Porter flew with me as my pilot in the right seat. I flew as the AC in the left seat, and I was the air mission commander for the CA. Our aircraft was also the C & C helicopter, so we would have the infantry battalion commander, a lieutenant colonel and some of his staff on our helicopter.

We landed at the airfield and went directly to the small Tactical Operations Center (TOC) in a tent not far from the runway. In the tent was the battalion commander, some of his staff, and a full colonel, who may have been the brigade commander. I never found out who he was. The staff was looking over a map board and started to explain what the plan was. Maj. Porter deferred to me to take the briefing. It was similar to what I had done many times before. When the briefing officer completed his presentation, I asked the questions we needed to know, such as exact number of troops to be lifted, how many would be in each stick for each aircraft, and to which LZ we would take which troops. We confirmed radio frequencies, artillery support and the time schedule. We locked down a number of other details. They asked how many helicopters we would have, because at that moment there was just my helicopter on the airfield. I assured him that the required lift ships would arrive shortly, and I told him the number of gunships we had coming in.

Soon the lift ships arrived and lined up beside the runway. They were from our company and some from other companies as well. We briefed the pilots on the mission and the information they would need. The infantry troops arrived and we loaded up. It was not long and we were in the air. The gunships were working with the flight, and we had contact with an Air Force FAC who would coordinate air strikes in support of the mission.

We would take the first load of troops to the first LZ and then go back to Kontum to pick up the second load to CA into the second LZ. In the distance, we could see air strikes hitting the first LZ, followed by the artillery fire going into the LZ. As the lead lift ship was on final for the LZ, the last artillery round went off and the gunships moved in to fire along the edges of the LZ to suppress any enemy fire that might come into play. Fortunately, the first lift went in without a hitch and the lift ships returned for the second lift.

I was on the radio coordinating with the flight leads for both the lift ships and the gunships. I was talking to the FAC about the next round of fast movers to come in for the second LZ. The battalion commander on my aircraft was able to talk to his unit commanders on the ground and all was going well for them. We would drop off the battalion commander as the last ship into the second LZ. Again, the air strikes hit the target, followed by artillery, followed by the gunships as the first lift ship made its approach. As the last lift ship was lifting out of the LZ, we came in and dropped off the battalion commander and his staff. As he climbed out of the helicopter, he came up and patted me on the shoulder with a big smile and said "thanks."

When we were clear of the LZ and all our aircraft were released from the mission to meet other mission requirements, Maj. Porter and I headed back to Camp Holloway. Throughout the entire operation he simply sat in his seat not saying a word; and, for part of the time, I turned the control of the aircraft over to him to fly. Finally, over the intercom, he looked over at me and said, "Will I ever learn how to do that?"

He did.

CHAPTER **24**

A Call From The Red Cross

THE AMERICAN RED Cross, or ARC, has been around a long time. ARC had a staff in Vietnam that supported U.S. troops. They shared many of the dangers of being in a combat zone and often risked their lives to help the soldiers.

The ARC staff's role had a number of different facets. The best known was the moral support provided by the young women, called "Donut Dollies." These women would provide light entertainment and audience participation programs for the soldiers. They served mostly at Red Cross recreation centers in-country, and at times would travel by helicopter or ground vehicle out to locations in the field to bring a touch of home to the soldiers.

I remember on at least one occasion flying a mission to carry a group of these women to a small base camp in the Highlands. They were all in Red Cross uniforms, and no matter how bad things were, they would try to cheer up the soldiers. Just their presence was an uplifting experience for the soldiers. Because they were American girls, they were referred to as "round eyes." I believe over the course of the war some of them became casualties, but I don't know the numbers. Just flying around in a helicopter in the combat zone was dangerous for them.

When the USO would put on entertainment shows in Vietnam with celebrities like Bob Hope, the Donut Dollies often accompanied them to provide help to the performers and support the troops. I never got to any of those shows, which most often were held in the large coastal bases, like Da Nang or Cam Ranh Bay. I stayed "up-country," rarely getting to the large base areas, and I never got into the city of Saigon during either of my tours.

Another significant function the Red Cross played was to assist with notifying soldiers of emergency situations with their families back in the States. A call from the Red Cross was always a call about something bad and a source of anxiety for anyone receiving one.

In late April, I was notified by the Red Cross that I had an emergency situation with my wife at home. The message came into my company headquarters and it stated that the family doctor was requesting my immediate return home because of an imminent serious operation that needed to be performed on my 2-year-old son. The situation was especially difficult because my wife was within weeks of giving birth to our third child. The Red Cross verified messages like this to ensure they were, in fact, truthful before they would notify the service member.

My new company commander, Maj. Randy Porter, was very concerned about me leaving at a time when we were conducting combat operations on a daily basis, and I was a key staff member as the operations officer. He and I talked well into the night when that message came in. In the end, he had the final authority to allow me to go or deny the request for my return home on emergency leave.

In our conversation as I remember it, we discussed who would be capable to take my place while I was gone. We both realized that the onset of the rainy season would have the effect of slowing combat operations in our area of operations (AO), so the need for me to run CAs would diminish in the coming months.

One of the principles the Army operated on was the principle of "fall out one," which meant that no matter what position you held, it was assumed you were not indispensable and the next in line in the chain of command could step up to replace you. That principle was particularly applicable to combat situations, in which key people often became casualties. In our conversation that evening, that point was discussed and we both knew that on any given day, I could become a casualty and the unit would have to continue to function without me.

Maj. Porter said he needed to sleep on it and he would give me his decision the next day. He decided to send me home, and I was enormously appreciative of that. He said since I knew the gravity of the situation at home, I would be terribly distracted and that might have a serious impact on my mission performance. I thanked him for his decision.

Orders were cut that set in motion the long journey back to the States that would eventually bring me to the Hillsboro Airport, near Providence, R.I., and a reunion with my wife and family.

There was great relief for my wife that I was able to return. She was near her wits' end trying to deal with the upcoming surgery on our son, which was to be at Boston Children's Hospital — about 40 miles from our home — as well as managing our daughter, and the nearness of the birth of our third child. What she had been dealing with was more than anyone should have to do alone. She is a very strong woman, but there is a limit for all of us and she was close to hitting her limit. No one could blame her — certainly not me.

It was a tumultuous time of dealing with doctors, meeting appointment schedules and providing for our daughter. People stepped in to help all along the way, including a Catholic monastery in Boston, with the nuns willing to allow my wife, our daughter and me to stay in the monastery for the duration of our son's stay in the hospital. Another group of nuns in a different monastery would take our daughter in during the day to care for her while we were at the hospital.

My memories of that period are a bit of a blur. I know the surgery was successful and our son was able to return home after two weeks in the hospital. There was hope that my wife would actually give birth while I was home, but the birth process was not advancing fast enough for that to happen. There were some who strongly suggested that Jean have the doctor induce the birth before I had to leave, but our doctor and Jean were opposed to forcing the birth.

I left to return to Vietnam before our third child — our second son — was born. Jean made me promise not to fly a helicopter again until I heard that our child had been born. I assured her that I would do as she asked, but I knew there was no way to keep that promise.

When I finally arrived back at the 119th, I again changed out of my khaki uniform and put my jungle fatigues back on. I was back in the air the next day flying missions in the AO. Maj. Porter was very glad to have me back. It was more than a week before I was notified that Jean had given birth to a beautiful, very large boy.

CHAPTER 25

Briefing At Dak Pek

THE MONSOON SEASON in the Highlands of central South Vietnam lasted from May into September, with the worst of it in the months of June, July and August. Heavy rain and low clouds made flying helicopters in the AO dicey at best, and near impossible at worst. There were many stories of pilots who crashed into the ground or mountains in perfectly good aircraft because they were caught in bad weather trying to get back to base when they would have been much better off remaining at another base until the weather improved. We used to call it "get-home-itis." It was responsible for the death of many flight crews and their passengers during the Vietnam War. Those deaths were all reported as accidents rather than combat-related.

It is hard to describe the intensity of the rain at times during the monsoon season. It seemed we could never get dry. Our clothes and feet were wet all the time. Moving by jeep or truck on the unimproved roads around Camp Holloway and Pleiku was often an exercise in frustration because of the mud and water.

The weather affected all combat operations for both the enemy and American / ARVN forces. We flew far fewer missions during this period, which left pilots and crews with considerable time on their hands, just waiting for a clear enough day to fly. Because I was the company operations officer, I spent a lot less time in the front seat of a helicopter. I would still take missions, but not nearly as many as I did when I was a platoon commander.

We didn't have any reliable navigation aids that would have the precision needed to fly in zero-visibility weather. Instrument Flight Rules (IFR) flying was very difficult and most pilots lacked the training and skill to safely fly in IFR conditions.

Some of the airfields had the capability to talk

you down through the clouds with what was known as a Ground Controlled Approach, or GCA. These GCA approaches were based on a radar system at the airfield that could identify an approaching aircraft, and an operator on the ground would talk to the pilot as he flew in for a landing. The controller would give commands based on the image on his radar scope and the pilot would follow the directions from the controller. The corrections provided by the controller were for aircraft heading, or direction, and rate of descent. If you were on the correct heading and on the correct glide path, a good controller could talk you down to the end of the runway with great precision. As pilots, we learned how to fly these approaches, and we would practice them in good weather.

Today the instrument landing systems are much more sophisticated and accurate, but we didn't have anything like them at that time.

The pilot had to have a great deal of skill and a lot of trust in the GCA controller when making a full IFR approach. You simply could not see anything through the windshield, it was all gray.

There was a time during my tour that the Army introduced a navigation system for our helicopters that was similar to what ships used at sea. It was based on a LORAN system, which used intersecting radio locations to fix your location. The system we had was called the Decca Navigator System, which allowed a pilot to know his position by receiving radio signals from fixed navigational beacons. A number of our helicopters had these Decca systems installed, with the intention that we would be able to fly in weather conditions that we would not otherwise fly in.

The Decca systems were delivered and installed at the end of the dry season so we could check the accuracy of them under good weather conditions. I flew with this system for a while. The claim was that the system was accurate enough to be able to locate the aircraft to within 50 to 60 feet for navigation purposes.

After testing these systems in clear weather, most of us agreed that we wouldn't trust them to have enough accuracy in the mountains to be safe. Reports of system malfunction for the Decca equipment pretty much ended the idea of using them for navigation in the mountains of

South Vietnam. These systems may have worked well in other areas, but not ours. I remember as the operations officer getting a lot of complaints from pilots and outright refusals to use them in actual IFR conditions. I wouldn't have, either.

On the Camp Holloway base, there was a small library containing some books that I think had been donated from the States. It was a small space carved out of an administrative building in the center of the compound. When I had time, I would go there to get a book to read. The soldier that ran it as a part-time duty got to know me and knew I liked history books, so whenever a new book came in, he would let me know. I would take the book back to my office, where there was decent light at night, and read at my desk sometimes late into the night. I learned a lot through that evening reading program in the summer of 1968.

We still conducted operations in the field when the weather permitted, and I remember an operation we had to plan for a CA in the mountains north of Dak To.

There was a small Special Forces camp with an

airstrip, called Dak Pek, about 20 km north of Dak To. Strung out along the border of Laos were a series of small camps manned by a few Special Forces soldiers and a number of indigenous soldiers, usually Montagnards. These teams were called A Teams, and they had the mission to conduct reconnaissance along the border and to report on enemy movements in their area. When they found evidence of enemy troop movement, it was often the intelligence needed to plan a CA into the area to locate and destroy the enemy units.

Being out in one of these little border camps was very risky and often they came under intense attacks by NVA forces. There were heroic stories of the A Teams fighting grossly outnumbered, resisting practically to the last man.

We got a tasker to conduct a CA near the border camp of Dak Pek, so I flew out to the camp to meet with the camp commander and to look at the area we would be using for an LZ. It was a rainy day, but the weather was clear enough for me to get there about mid-day.

I landed my helicopter just off the runway, close

to a bunker complex that was the operations center for the camp. I left my helicopter running with my pilot sitting in the right seat as I climbed out to meet the camp commander. A Special Forces captain came out of the bunker to meet me about halfway between my helicopter and the bunker. As we stood there talking about the upcoming CA, the camp suddenly came under 122 mm rocket attack. It was sudden and violent. Before we had a chance to move, a 122 mm rocket hit the hill right beside us, not 10 feet away. Miraculously for the two of us, the rocket didn't detonate on impact. It went deep into the soft mud of the hill, creating a perfect hole, but not blowing up.

I signaled my pilot to take off until the attack was over, and I followed the SF captain into his bunker. The attack only lasted about 15 minutes, with several rockets landing beside the airstrip and exploding. When it was over, I continued my briefing with the captain in the bunker and then used his radio to call my helicopter back in. I climbed into my helicopter and we headed back to Camp Holloway. The next day, I flew the C&C helicopter for a company-sized CA just west of the Dak Pek Camp without any major incidents or enemy contact. I believe it was June 11, and my flight records indicate that I flew 11 hours that day.

I am sure some of the 122 mm rockets fired at us during the time I was in Vietnam were duds, but I had never heard of one before the incident at Dak Pek.

According to my flight records, my final flight in South Vietnam was on Oct. 8. I remember the flight. I was getting close to my DEROS, which was scheduled for Oct. 14. I already had a "turtle" as my replacement as the company operations officer. A mission tasker came down for an administrative flight to take five or six passengers from the Pleiku airbase to Lane Army Airfield in Binh Dinh Province, just west of the coastal city of Qui Nhon. I took the tasker and the next day flew over to the airbase to pick up the passengers. As we took off from the Pleiku airbase that day, it was a clear, beautiful, sunny day, so I was not anticipating any weather issues for the flight. Lane Airfield was reporting good weather also, with a report of a few clouds in the Mang Yang Pass, which is where Route 19 cut through the mountains and was about the halfway mark for our flight.

We were flying pretty high that day at about 5,000 feet above ground level. Our flight path pretty much followed the highway as it wound up through the mountains, headed for the sea and Qui Nhon.

I do not remember who was flying with me that day, but I was flying in the left seat as the AC for the mission. As we came up on the pass, the views of the green-covered mountains were beautiful. We were able to see the impressions in the ground on the side of the mountain that marked the grave sites for the French soldiers who had been part of Group Mobile 100 and killed in a large ambush near the end of the French Indochina War. Bernard Fall wrote about the event in his famous book, "Street Without Joy: The French Debacle in Indochina." I read most of Fall's books while I was in Vietnam.

As we flew east through the pass, we were not far from Camp Radcliff, where the 173rd Airborne Brigade was stationed at An Khe. Although there were a few clouds, the weather was not an issue that day.

About 20 minutes from arriving at Lane Army Airfield, my crew chief called me on the intercom to report that he smelled fuel in the cabin. The door gunner also reported smelling fuel. I told them to make sure all our passengers put out any cigarettes they may have been smoking. The crew chief started taking off the interior panels so he could get a visual check of the engine compartment. The news was not good. He reported that we had fuel running all over the engine deck, with no obvious indication of where it was coming from.

We all knew that if the fuel had come in contact with any of the really hot engine areas, we would quickly become a big orange ball in the sky. I called Lane Airfield and declared an emergency and asked that crash equipment be made available for my landing. I also told them we had a fuel leak and needed to expedite our approach into the airfield rather than follow the normal landing traffic pattern.

We did not tell the passengers the nature of the

problem only that they were not to light up any cigarettes for the remainder of the flight. It was very tense, and I flew the helicopter as fast as it could go and descended in a direct approach to the airfield. We could see the crash equipment assembling beside the runway as we came in.

As soon as we got the skids on the ground, I shut down the aircraft and everyone quickly exited. The firemen came up to the aircraft with their hoses ready, but there never was a fire. After the helicopter was shut down for a while, the maintenance officer from the helicopter unit assigned to Lane came over to look at the aircraft with a couple of technicians from his team. They were able to find the source of the leak; it was a fuel line.

It took a couple of hours to make the necessary repairs, then the maintenance officer took the helicopter up for a test flight. After he landed and inspected the aircraft, he signed off on the log book that the aircraft was safe to fly. We cranked it up and headed back to Camp Holloway without any more incidents or difficulties. I remember how close we were to a disaster.

That was the last flight of my first tour in Vietnam. Within days, I signed out of the 119th and it was my turn to get on a "freedom" bird to fly home.

Maj. Randy Porter was, like Joe Campbell, a good man and a good commander. I have copied the comment section of the OER he wrote on me below.

OER written by Warren R. Porter, MAJ, CE 119th AHC Company Commander — 23 October 1968. (This statement has been reproduced exactly as the original, signed copy that I have in my files.)

"CPT Heslin performed his duties as operations officer in a combat environment in a most outstanding manner. Through his keen insights and thorough knowledge of all phases of combat operations involving an assault helicopter company he was able to guide junior officers in the accomplishment of their missions in such a manner that this unit constantly received praise for the professional manner in which it participated in combat assault operations. As Aviation Safety Officer he was directly responsible for the outstanding aviation safety record of 353 accident free flying days set by this unit. CPT Heslin's devotion to duty and sense of urgency have set an example for others to follow. He was an invaluable asset to this unit and the United States Army."

Captain John G. "Jack" Heslin home from the first tour.

CHAPTER **26**

In The Mail

WHEN I WAS in Vietnam, there were really only two ways to communicate with loved ones back home. There was, of course, the mail service. The other means of communicating was through the use of the Military Auxiliary Radio System (MARS). The program allowed service members in Vietnam to contact their families in the United States through a combination of telephone and amateur radio operators in the States. Usually the service member had to schedule the MARS call through a facility on a base. That meant if they were out in the field, they really had no way to use the MARS system. However, when they got back to their base camp they often could schedule a call.

At Camp Holloway, we had an opportunity to schedule calls through the MARS system. To do that, we had to schedule a time and then report to a communications bunker, where there would be a field phone with which you could call over to Pleiku Air Force Base. There, they had the facilities to make a MARS connection. Those calls were limited to about five minutes because there was a considerable demand for the calls and the service was not always available.

The call went out by high-frequency radio from Vietnam — in our case Pleiku — to a volunteer amateur radio operator in the United States. That operator was able to patch the radio call into the regular commercial phone system in the States. It was a bit dicey at times because the high-frequency radios they used depended on the high altitude weather conditions, which could change rapidly, even in the middle of a call.

It was an enormous boost to be able to talk to your wife back home. We all looked forward to the opportunity to make a MARS call and I was fortunate enough to make several during my tour.

Using the MARS system was not like making a call in the States. Because one leg of the call was through a ham radio operator, it was necessary for the operator to listen to the call so he could switch back and forth between the two people speaking. It was an asynchronous call, in that it was not automatic like a normal phone call. Each time one party in the call was finished speaking, they had to say the word "over," which was the signal for the operator to switch over to the other party on the line. As a result, you might have a call in which you said, "Hi honey, I love you — over." Even though it was an aggravation, it was the closest we could come to direct contact with loved ones. Sometimes if there was a family emergency, the Red Cross could step in to establish a priority and the service member could be bumped to the head of the call schedule.

During the time I spent in South Vietnam on my first tour, I was fortunate to receive many letters from my wife and some from family members. Without a doubt, mail was a very important factor for the morale of the soldiers. Great efforts were made to get mail out to the troops, no matter where they were. It was the connection to home, and for many, a connection to a saner world than the one they were living in. Some soldiers did not receive much mail and there were efforts to have people from home send letters that could be distributed to any soldier, especially those not receiving many letters.

In late December 1967, I received a large manila envelope from my brother-in-law, Bill Evans, who was an eighth-grade teacher at East Hartford High School. It was just before Christmas and Bill had given his students a homework assignment to write a letter to a soldier in Vietnam. Bill told them about me and that I was a helicopter pilot in Vietnam.

There were 25 student letters in the package. I still have the package and all the letters. Rereading them provided me an interesting insight into the "climate of opinion" in late 1967 as seen through the eyes of 13-year-old students. I was not able to answer each student, but I did send a letter back to Bill thanking the class for their efforts and support. I have reprinted all 26 letters, to include Bill's letter, and put them in an appendix at the back of this book.

I sent out letters to my family as often as I could, especially to my wife. I have retained most of the letters sent to me in Vietnam from family and friends. Those letters brought the reality of another world back home that was real and not filled with the horrors we witnessed daily. The letters in some way were like a life ring for someone who felt like he was drowning.

The last letter I wrote on my first tour was on Oct. 10, 1968. I wrote it to my parents. Years later, the letter was found by my sisters who were cleaning out my parents' house after my father died. They found it among some "precious" items my mother had kept. My sister sent me the letter. I have reproduced it here as a way to convey what I was thinking as I ended my first combat tour.

"Dear Mom & Dad,

I think this will be the last letter I have to write from Viet Nam. I wanted to write this letter to tell you what wonderful parents you are. You are an outstanding example for the rest of us to live up to. You have taught us all the true meaning of love and the real values to live by.

How often I have thought of things you have said — advice you have given that has shaped my life. What I am — whatever I may do — you can honestly say is what you have made of me. Today the difficulties of bringing up children almost seem insurmountable yet, I can see by what you have done — with the help of God children can be brought up to know, love and serve God.

Mom & Dad, you can take great joy and satisfaction in the knowledge that because you two grand people have been here, this world is a better place to live. Please God I pray that my children love and respect me as I do my parents.

God Love and Bless you.
Your loving Son,
Jack

No matter what horror we may see — no matter what hardships may befall us. Life can be so beautiful when seen through love tinted glasses."

10 Oct 68.

Dear Mom & Dad,
        I think this will be the last
letter I have to write from Viet Nam.
I want to write this letter to tell
you what wonderful parents you are.
You are an outstanding example for the
rest of us to live up to. You have taught
us all the true meaning of love and the
real values to live by. How often I have
thought of things you have said — advice
you have given that has shaped my
life. What I am — what ever I may
do — you can honestly say is what
you have made of me. Today the
difficulties of bringing up children almost
seem insurmountable yet — I can see
by what you have done — with
the help of God children can be brought
up to know, love & serve God.
        Mom & Dad, you can take great
joy and satisfaction in the knowledge
that because you two grand people

have been here, this world is a
better place to live. Please God
I pray that my children love and
respect me as I do my parents.
God Love and Bless you.

                    Your loving son,
                    Jack XX

No matter what horror we may see
no matter what hardships may befall
us.
Life can be so beautiful when seen
through love tinted glasses.

CHAPTER **27**

Reflections

AFTER MORE THAN 50 years, it has been an interesting journey to revisit events of my past that had held so much fear, anxiety and mystery for me. For so many years, I could not talk about my first tour in Vietnam because I thought I would be like Humpty Dumpty falling off a wall with nobody to put me back together again.

There are many combat veterans, from many wars, who have had to deal with the things they witnessed and the things they did. It has been the plight of soldiers across history and across cultures.

The Vietnam War was a divisive event in American history. Some have said it is the most divisive event in Modern American history. I would agree with that.

Looking back through the years, I have seen the impact of that war on many people and on our culture.

There was one narrative in America after WWII: it was a "good war" where American sacrifices saved the world from the evil of Nazism, Fascism and Japanese imperialism. Since there was only one narrative, there was no divisiveness about the story. Similarly, there was only one narrative about the Korean War: America saved the people of South Korea from the onslaught of Communist North Korea. That narrative has prevailed for all these years, and the evidence of contemporary South Korea supports that.

However, there are two competing narratives in American culture about the Vietnam War. One, which is the dominant narrative, is that it was a "bad war" and that America is guilty of visiting death and horror on the people of Vietnam. Those who believe this narrative say we never should have intervened in Indo China, specifically Vietnam.

The other narrative is that it was a noble effort, not unlike that in Korea, to save the Vietnamese people of the Republic of South Vietnam from the assaults by the Communists from North Vietnam, and to preserve freedom for the South Vietnamese not unlike what the rest of the Western World enjoys.

These two competing narratives persist today and have festered for all these years creating a cultural divide that I don't expect to see healed during my lifetime.

Like most veterans, I lived my war just as each veteran lived his or her own war. They were not the same. When someone says, "I know all about the Vietnam War" because he or she saw a movie about it, many of us are disappointed that the depth of understanding, for many, seems to be just a veneer.

My hope in sharing my story here is that someone will read it and gain a little more insight into what that experience was like, and then look for more information to   better understand the entire events of that period.

Members of the Vietnam War generation, like all the previous war generations, are passing off the stage of life quickly. For Vietnam veterans, exposure to Agent Orange is accelerating the process. If the painful sacrifices made by my generation, often in blood, have any value to subsequent generations, then the following generations must seek out the truth and learn the lessons for which we paid dearly. Only time will tell what the world of my children and grandchildren will look like. Many of us stood in the fire on battlefields across the world so that later generations of Americans would have the freedoms we had. May God bless America.

Appendix A — Careers

MILITARY CAREER

Lt. Col. Heslin was born in 1943 in Woonsocket, R.I., and attended high school at La Salle Academy. He graduated from Providence College in Providence, R.I., with a Bachelor of Arts degree in sociology and was commissioned in the U.S. Army, June 1965. He attended Infantry Officer Basic Course and Airborne Training at Fort Benning, Ga., and was assigned to the 82nd Airborne Division, in which he served as a platoon leader in the Dominican Republic and commanded the rear detachment for 1st Battalion, 504th Infantry at Fort Bragg, N.C.

Lt. Col. Heslin attended Rotary Wing Flight School from October 1966 through June 1967. As an Army aviator, he was assigned to the 57th Assault Helicopter Company at Fort Bragg, N.C.

and deployed with the unit to Vietnam in October 1967. Upon arrival in Vietnam, he was assigned to the 119th Assault Helicopter Company, in which he served as an assault helicopter platoon commander and operations officer.

Following completion of his first tour in Vietnam, Jack was assigned to the U.S. Army Aviation Center at Fort Rucker, Ala., where he performed duties as a senior instructor for the Warrant Officer Career Course and commanded the 31st Enlisted Student Company. After completing the Infantry Officer Advanced Course as an honor graduate in July 1971, he attended Fixed Wing Transition Training en route to his second tour in Vietnam from December 1971 through December 1972. In Vietnam, he performed duties as the 52nd Combat Aviation Battalion S-3, operations officer, and later Assistant S-3 for the 17th Combat Aviation Group.

Upon returning from Vietnam in December 1972, Lt. Col. Heslin enrolled in the University of Rhode Island as a master's degree candidate in the Department of Sociology. He received his master's degree and graduated with honors in 1974. He immediately assumed duties as an ROTC instructor at the University of Rhode Island, where he served for three years.

In 1977, he was selected for attendance at the Naval War College Command and Staff Course and graduated with honors in June 1978.

After aviator refresher training at Fort Rucker, Ala., Jack reported into the 3d Squadron, 4th Cavalry, 25th Infantry Division, HI, October 1978. He served as the 3d Squadron S-3 for one year and as commander of C Troop for one year before joining Headquarters Western Command as the Aviation Officer, DCSOPS, in December 1980.

Jack was assigned to Fort Lee, Va., in August 1981 as the Chief, Operations & Tactics Branch, of the Unit Training Directorate, U.S. Army Logistics Center. He later served as the Division Chief for the Current Exercise Division and special projects officer before retiring on Dec. 31, 1985.

Jack has had a number of articles published in professional military journals.

Lt. Col. Heslin has been awarded the Silver Star,

the Distinguished Flying Cross, the Bronze Star Medal with oak leaf cluster, the Air Medal with V device and 24 oak leaf clusters, the Meritorious Service Medal with three oak leaf clusters, Army Commendation Medal, Army Achievement Medal, Presidential Unit Citation (Army), National Defense Service Medal, Vietnam Service Medal, Armed Forces Expeditionary Medal, Army Service Ribbon and Overseas Service Ribbon.

CIVILIAN CAREER

Until August 2002, Jack was the Coordinator for Workforce Development at John Tyler Community College (JTCC) in Chester, Va. Jack had been with the Virginia Community College System as a sociology professor and an administrator at JTCC with the responsibility for apprenticeship programs and the operation of the Outreach Centers at Fort Lee and Midlothian Va. He has worked extensively with companies and secondary schools in the greater Richmond metropolitan area as they participated with John Tyler Community College in developing the workforce through public-private partnerships.

Jack has made numerous presentations on workforce development to area, state and national educators and business leaders. He has appeared before several state-level appropriations and finance committees.

After leaving John Tyler Community College and becoming a workforce development consultant, Jack became part of the Thinking Media team and for more than eight years served as the in-state representative for KeyTrain in the state of Virginia.

Jack was a founding member of the Chester Rotary Club and is a life member of the Vietnam Helicopter Pilots Association VHPA, the VFW and the Distinguished Flying Cross Society.

Author of the award winning website "The Battle of Kontum," and, the book "Reflections From the Web."

Appendix B - Student Letters

In December 1967, my brother-in-law Bill Evans' eighth-grade class at East Hartford High School, Connecticut, sent me 25 letters his students had written as a homework assignment. The letters were addressed to "a soldier in Vietnam" or they were addressed to me.

I reprinted Bill's letter to me below. I also republished the student letters but I have omitted the last names of the students.

"December 19, 1967

Dear Jack,

Congratulations on your promotion to Captain. Enclosed are a series of letters which some of my 8th grade students wrote. I thought that you might get a kick out of them. They're nice kids and wrote these at home and brought them in.

In just less than a week, Christmas will be upon us. We'll miss having you home, but with God's blessings, perhaps, we can all get together next year. The kids are higher than kites lately; they can't wait until the 25th.

We plan on heading for R.I. on Christmas day and will stay a few days. God Bless you, Jack; have a Merry Christmas.

Love,
Bill"

"Dear Captain Heslin

This is the first time I have written to someone in Vietnam. How are things going over there? Are things real rough were (sic) you are now?

I understand that you're a helicopter pilot. What type of helicopters do you fly?

Everybody around here is getting ready for Christmas. Around were (sic) I live people have all their Christmas lights on outside their houses.

The football season for East Hartford High was pretty bad we lost all but one game. Usually we're the number one team and take the CDC championship but things were just the opposite.

Sincerely,
Dave B"

"Dear Captain Heslin,

As you know I'm an eighth grader at East Hartford High School so I'll tell you something else about myself like school very much and my favorite subjects are the one I do best in are Spanish and American history. I have two sisters and three brothers and I am hurt.

I'd like to tell you what a good job the soldiers in Vietnam are doing. I think you are doing the right thing helping the people of South Vietnam. I hope the soldiers keep trying their hardest to help these people.

If you get a chance to answer this letter please tell me more about yourself. I now must close my letter and even if I'm late in wishing you a Merry Christmas and a Happy New Year

Sincerely,
Susan B"

"Dear Captain Heslin,

Being a supporter of the American policy on Vietnam, I was more than happy
to have the chance to communicate with
someone who is right there. I have always
wanted to become an Air Force officer
when it is my turn to serve my country,
and since you are a pilot, I jumped at the
opportunity to write to you.

After viewing some television docu-
mentaries, I have received only a slight
impression of the fighting in Vietnam,
but enough to see that many soldiers
are disturbed by the reports of demonstrations, draft card burning, and the
like. These anti-war exhibitions should
not concern you men, because perhaps
at the most, three or five per cent of the
United States' population is actually
against the war. Some people may dif-
fer in their views on how it is handled,
but let's not forget there have been
"hawks" and "doves" in every war.

From the little experience I've had with
logical thinking, I reasoned a possible

theory as to why there is anti-war representation in our country. Because of man's nature, there were always demonstrations and petitions against every war, but because of the lack of communications, no one ever heard of those people, and the tyrannical rule of most countries put down most uprisings, even some peaceful ones. On the other hand, I believe that when the democratic type of government was introduced in the United States, the people were given much more freedom than in earlier civilizations. Realizing this, some American extremists began to present objections about almost all Federal decisions. As if this was not enough, Communists have definitely been the cause of some modern draft card destruction and anti-war protests. But please don't worry yourselves, because you men still have the full cooperation and backing of just about the entire United States of America. Doesn't that make you feel proud?

Sincerely yours,
George D"

"To a soldier in Vietnam,

Hi, my name is Debbie and I am thirteen years old in the eighth grade at East Hartford High School. I thought I would write to a soldier, even though we haven't met because we all get lonely sometimes.

I want to tell you that I really appreciate what you are doing in Vietnam. I know, too, that the people of the United States are proud of our men.

The people here and myself know what you are fighting for; to stop the spread of communism. I hope and know you men will accomplish this task.

Sincerely yours,
Debra D"

"Dear Captain Heslin,

I picked to write to you because I feel I know how the situation over in Vietnam is. My brother just came back from Vietnam in which he was over there for a year.

He wrote and told us never to stop writing because letters is what keeps the guys going. By writing letters you can relieve some of the pain of the war.

First I will tell you what it is like over here and what is happening at the moment. It is almost Christmas and there is still no snow on the ground. It's cold but I guess not cold enough. Everyone is busy buying gifts, sending cards, etc. There are dances and parties practically all the time. But don't think for a moment any one forgets about you men. The people are always thinking about you guys.

You're doing a great job. I hope you don't have too much more time over there because I'm sure there are people waiting for your return.

I'm writing this as an English assignment and I hope we don't get marked. If we do I'll get an F because I'm a lousy writer. I guess you have guessed that by now. Well I think I better close now so I can finish my homework. Bye

(P.S. I hope you never run out of gas.)

Ha! Ha!

Yours truly,
Nancy D"

"Dear Captain Heslin,

I am a thirteen year old boy living on a small street in a residential section of East Hartford, Connecticut.

Things around here can get pretty dull at times, but every now and then something exciting will happen such as a fire or a tree falling down.

According to the newspapers and television I can imagine how rough things are out there. You must get discouraged hearing about all the draft card burners and voters protesting the war.

I think that the men fighting in Viet Nam are doing a good job in stopping the flow of Communism from spreading around the world.

Yours truly,
Ray D"

"To a soldier in Vietnam,

I want to tell you an honest opinion of what most people feel about Vietnam. We all realize the necessity of your being there, and we are real proud of you. Your (sic) really serving your country in one of the most honorable ways I know. The nuts that run around burning draft cards are certainly not doing much for the United States' reputation.

I've been reading in newspapers and magazines that a letter from the Unites States is quite a morale booster. I'm not much for writing letters, but if this letter serves any good, it's doing its purpose. It's really hard to believe that this letter that I'm writing will really be read in Vietnam by a soldier, but I have no idea of what to say. Even now my choice of conversation seems far from interesting.

I'm an eighth grader and I attend the East Hartford High School. You'd be surprised how much the upperclassmen resent us being here. The school is real nice though, and I enjoy being here. (most of the time). We really miss the eighth grade sports, because some of the clubs don't allow eighth graders.

I know it's probably impossible for you to write back, but I would be very happy to receive a letter from you.

Sincerely,
Sue D"

"Dear Captain John G. Heslin

I am writing to say what a great job the American men have done in Viet Nam. I, for one, believes this war necessary to fight.

I want to tell you a little about my family and myself. As you know, I'm an eight grade student in the East Hartford High School and I like it very much although the seniors found it a little hard to get used to us. I belong to a family of seven, four sisters and my parents, and I must not forget our dog, Spot. Things get a little wild at our home many times but nothing that can't be controlled.

I enjoyed writing to you and if you have time please write back. I wanted to know what you feel about the war.

Sincerely yours,
Kathy G"

"To a Soldier in Vietnam,

In starting my letter I would like to say why I am writing. Captain John Heslin's brother-in-law, Mr. William Evans, is one of my teachers. He teaches us History, English, and Literature. For an English assignment we are to write a letter to Captain Heslin and he in turn will distribute them among his men. I hope to continue this correspondence with you further than the boundary of an English assignment.

I am for the American cause in Vietnam and I am well aware of what and why you are fighting this conflict for. The people who remonstrate the war are not doing you a good job in building morale.

To tell about myself is easy. My name is Paul H. and I am 13. I go to East Hartford High School in the accelerated eighth grade. I'm about 5'5" and I weigh close to 110 pounds. Enclosed you will find a picture of me. If you want to write me, my address is:

Paul H
38 Mary Street
East Hartford, 8, Connecticut 06108

In your letter tell me where you are from and what your address is. I would appreciate if you could tell me about yourself.

Sincerely yours,
Paul H"

"Dear Captain

Judging from all these protests and war demonstrations you might have the question, is fighting in Vietnam. You should not let these people even bother you in the least. These people are remonstrating for something that they know little or nothing about. I know that this kind of behavior can be discouraging, knowing that some Americans don't want the United States in the Vietnam War. It can even be more distracting if these are protests by people who aren't even interested in the war at all.

I'm a firm believer about the war. It is very implicit that in my mind and more than likely armies of other people feel the same way. If we pull out of the war Communism would keep on spreading until it could rule the world. The next thing the Americans would know is it would be knocking on our own United States.

I know sometimes the war can be quite

unbearable. People over here can sometimes be extremely weird. They put gasoline on them and burn themselves for no reason at all. It can be quite discouraging for the soldiers who are over in Vietnam. Well, I must start my History so your brother in law Mr. Evans, won't get upset and the studying will help me in my test tomorrow.

Sincerely yours,
Bill H"

"Dear Soldier,

I am writing you because I believe in what you're doing and would like to help as much as possible. I feel that by writing this letter I am helping to remind you that people are always thinking about and thanking you for what you are doing.

I think I should tell you a little about

myself so you may understand what kind of person I am. I go to the 8th grade I am 13 I like cars.

I would like you to write if possible the address is

Durfee H
1677 Main Street
East Hartford 8 Connecticut 06108

I would like to know what it's really like over there.

Sincerely yours,
Durfee H"

"To all the G.I.s around at the time of mail call:

I am a thirteen year old boy, in the eighth grade attending East Hartford High School, or known around here as E.H.H.S. Owning a newspaper route

I have a working knowledge of many matters and since I like to know what's going on I keep pretty well informed about the world events and I follow the news about Vietnam and what's going on.

First on the list of things I would like to tell you that I am 100%, well, maybe not 100% but at least 99.9% behind you guys in this war you are fighting over there, and that if I get a chance to fight in the very same war I shall go willing and not like some of the college students over here burning their Draft Cards and protesting. It seems all they are really looking for is their name in the paper and the publicity. Actually, to be truthful with you I do not fully understand what this war is all about or how it started but for some reason I feel the reasons must be pretty close to what this country was fighting about way back in 1776, somehow you don't seem to need a reason for trying to stay free and able to speak as you wish. I honestly hope that people will begin to realize that in this crazy-mixed up world in order to keep our freedom and our country free of narrow-minded communists we have to be over in that part of the world letting them understand that we are willing to protect our interests.

Another topic that is on my mind is this, I know that you guys like to receive letters from the States and me with my wander-mind was trying to think of a way I could get a correspondence started with at least one of you who is interested in a pen pal sort of thing. The more interested in writing to me the better I know some of you won't be able to but those who do I'll send clippings of the old home team to each of you and anything that might be of interest to you if you let me know. I hope I get a good response and I'll return it double.

Another thing just in case I'm unable to get another letter off before next week,

I certainly wish each and every one of you the Merriest of Christmas's and of course a New Years which will better for all of you.

I have many interests, you name them and I usually have a finger trying them, reading, playing the accordion, models collecting coins some to spend and some to save for a rainy day you know what I mean. So hoping to hear from some of you soon.

Very Sincerely Yours,
Ron J"

"To a soldier in Viet Nam,

I am very happy that I have the pleasure of righting (sic) to a soldier. Because I think you are in Viet Nam for a very good cause. All our 8th grade class is writing to some soldier's in Viet Nam. We hope that everyone does this because we know it must be hard to keep the moral of all the soldiers high.

Now let me tell you about myself. I am thirteen years old and in eighth grade. The city I live in is East Hartford and go to East Hartford High School. In my family I have one brother, one sister, mother, father and a beagle dog. My sister is only 10 and my brother is 6. I am the oldest in the family.

Right now we are preparing for Christmas. You should see the beautiful Christmas lights on Constitution Plaza in Hartford. They would be even prettier if we had some snow. I suppose we will have some snow for Christmas.

I hope that you and all the soldiers will be home for Christmas 1968

Yours truly,
Vicky J"

"To a Soldier in Vietnam,

Hi, I am twelve years old, in the eighth grade and I go to East Hartford High School. I like school excepting a few subjects such as Algebra and History. They would be interesting if you understood them. You would'nt (sic) believe the marks I have in History. My report card wasn't that terrific either.

Right now it's beautiful outside (that is for this time of year) It's already December 14, almost winter! My birthday is December 19, and I will finally be 13 years old.

Around our neighborhood it is very quiet (excepting me). I have a few girlfriends around here but most of the kids are boys in college.

I guess I'll tell you some more about myself. I love fruit (especially oranges and grapfruits (sic)) My favorite sports are basketball and soccer. I don't only like to watch them being played but I like to play them.

Hope you enjoyed my letter and guess I'll let you go. I'll wright (sic) again and I hope you get my letter.

Sincerely Yours,
Susan L"

"Dear Captain Heslin,

It doesn't look as though we're going to have a white Christmas this year. In fact, the kind of weather that we are having now is more appropriate for March. I want to have a Christmas where big fluffy snowflakes fall all day.

I don't think the bells that I wear on my shoes are going to help me get into the Christmas spirit, but since there is no snow I've got to do something! I suppose I could get our ice crusher out and attempt to make some artificial snow, but that would be rather absurd.

No matter what any naïve person says about "pulling out" of Vietnam, there are a hundred others who say that we should stay. We must try to understand those unfortunates who can't see the purpose of remaining there. These are the ones who we should not hold them responsible for what they say.

Merry Christmas and may God bless you all,
Claudia L"

"Dear Captain Heslin,

From the few things Mr. Evans mentioned about you and from what I see on the television you soldiers in the helicopeter (sic) are doing a great job. The television shows the soldiers going in the middle of a conflict and send supplies and men or taking the wounded out. You also have many rockets which you fire at "Charlie". I think the soldiers like you help very much in the war. From being a Captain you must run most of these platoons.

My cousin, Butch, is leaving for Vietnam January third and is going to guard a prison for the captured enemies. Butch is home now for a month before he leaves. When I talk to him he says that he is glad to help out and that the boys or men that go to Vietnam really learn to be a man before they go back home.

I know a little about how you soldiers camp and have camp packs to carry. I've been on many camping trips up north with older teen-agers. In my back yard and all around my neighborhood there are many woods about five square miles in size. My friends and I hunt with bows and guns during the summer and set out for a day for fishing. I know it's nothing like you do but it tells you the kind of person I am.

Good luck,
Frank M"

"Dear Captain,

Hi Captain Heslin of the 119th Assault Airborne, or something like that. I just thought I'd write and tell you how things are around here.

First I will tell you about myself. My favorite sport is football, and the Baltimore Colts are my heroes of the Professional Football World. I am 13 yrs. Old, my birthday is Saturday December 16. I am a boy, in case you didn't know yet.

I think about Vietnam quite a lot and I do sincerely believe we should be in Vietnam. Communism should definitely be stopped, along with the Vietcong. Keep up the good work!

I enjoy fooling around with boys and girls, especially girls of course. Well, I guess I'll be leaving now so I can go fool around with some more girls, byeeeeee (sic)

Very Sincerely Yours,
Guy S. N"

"Dear soldier,

I am pleased and honored to be writing to a man whose efforts are helping to protect our nation. By stopping the spread of communism, you soldiers will keep us safe in the future. You are doing a great job. Keep up the good work.

My name is Judy and I live in East Hartford, Connecticut. My hobbies are skiing, skating, and swimming. Enjoying dramatics, I played the part of "Gretl" in the "Sound of Music". I like all sports.

What are the thirteen year old Vietnamese children like? I would sure like to know about them. If you have a chance would you write and tell me about them? Please write back to me and tell be about Viet Nam.

Your friend,
Judith N"

"To a Soldier in Vietnam,

Hi! This is the first letter I've ever written to a soldier but I hope it's not my last. I'm a girl and my name is Chris. If you receive this before Christmas, I hope you have a wonderful one and I send my most sincere wishes. It's really cold here in Connecticut but we haven't had much snow. That's fine with me because I have to shovel it since my brother is away. He's in the U.S. Coast Guard Academy and I'm very proud of him because it's the biggest thing he's ever done and he's sticking to it.

What is your job while your (sic) there? I'm kind of lucky; none of my family or friends have gone yet. But it really hurts when you here (sic) how the soldiers are dying. I'm all for the war, though, because I know they're doing it for their country. There's a song out called "An

Open Letter to My Teenage Son" and the last line goes "If you burn your draft card, burn your birth certificate too, because from that moment on, I have no son." After that, I get all emotional and start crying. First I'm emotional and secondly I'm proud to be an American. I know that since you are there, you're just as proud as me and just as willing to fight for it.

Well I have to close my letter since I have no more to say. So again I wish you a very Merry Christmas.

Very Sincerely Yours,
Chris P

P.S.
If you have time, could you please write back? Thank you, Bye again."

"Dear Captain Heslin,

I am writing because I want you to know just about everyone is behind you men in Viet Nam. People in America can't thank you enough for what you are doing. There are a few "draft card burners" but these "men" don't deserve to be called Americans anyway.

I am on eighth grade student and at home my father often talks about protestors. Everyone should be proud of every American in Viet Nam. Fortunately most people are. There is only a small percentage of protesters but newspapers make it seem like there are so many. Even though I'm only in the eigth (sic) grade I go to the high school in East Hartford. There is a great advantage of going to high school such as a nice gym and good equipment, but when you're thirteen in a high school you're real small.

Sincerely yours,
John P"

"Dear Captain,

This letter is not to make you homesick, but to tell you what is going on here in Connecticut. Winter is just around the corner here and it is still nice weather out. The average temperature of today was 50.

Being an eighth grader in a high school does have its disadvantages. I am small and walking through a corridor with tall seniors in it doesn't please me. Well that's enough about me.

The situation toward Vietnam shows that we are for you. The demonstrators, what few there are, shouldn't bother you. I know and I both hope the fighting is over soon and I also know that you are doing your best job. The fighting is for a good cause. I hope this war stops the spread of Communism.

Yours truly,
Mark P"

"Dear Captain Heslin

Here in Connecticut everything and everybody is bustling with Christmas Spirit! There's a lot of colorful lights, beautiful trees and many little tots with hopes of Christmas. If you walk down Main Street in Hartford you will see people of all shapes and sizes doing all kinds of shopping, but they have one thing in common, their smiling!

As you have guessed from this letter, I'm a girl and I don't really know very much about the war in Vietnam. But I do know one thing, the men fighting there for their country are really great and deserve a lot of regignition (sic). People in the United States that are old enough to know what the war is all about, are really thankful to you for what you're doing for us.

Sincerely yours,
Sharon P"

"Dear Captain,

Judging by your position in Vietnam, I expect the war to last until 1972. When will your superiors start something big!!!! I hope it is very soon to end the war, and bring you soldiers back home, and commend you for the wonderful job you have done.

Recently I have been into downtown Hartford to see the "Festival of Lights." It is a beautiful sight to see, and all persons believe praise is the word to the people who set up the "Festival of Lights."

My name is Jeff R. I am 5 feet 10 inches tall, 135 pounds, like all types of sports, and very ambitious. I have medals and trophies for swimming, basketball, baseball, football, bowling and hockey. Sometime in the distant future I hope to meet you man-to-man and talk about the war in Vietnam. I also hope to end the war in Vietnam as I have stated.

Sincerely yours,
Jeff R"

"Dear Captain Heslin,

My teacher has informed me that you are the pilot of a helicopter. I have always liked helicopters, and I long to ride in one.

I have a book on helicopters and I can just imagine the one which you pilot. It would give me great pride in knowing that I rescued wounded soldiers, as you do.

I can just imagine, you and I zooming over the land, spotting men in distress, going down to pick them up, and then "tear" back to a hospital. But I don't think we'll get our chance, because the men over there are fighting such a great battle, the whole thing ought to be over soon.

I want to wish you the best of luck in all the years to come, also a very Merry Christmas and a Happy New Year.

Sincerely Yours,
Steve S"

"To a soldier in Vietnam,

The soldiers over there are doing a great job. I feel that our being in the war is right.

There is really nothing good happening around here. Since Christmas is coming the lights are going on in Constitution Plaza in Hartford.

In my family there's my mother, father, sister and me. Everybody's good to me especially my sister who is nineteen.

Well I hope you have a very merry Christmas and a happy New Year.

A friend in the States,
Kathy S"

Appendix C — Specifications (UH-1H) Helicopter

General characteristics

- **Crew:** 1—4

- **Capacity:** 3,880 pounds including 14 troops, or 6 stretchers, or equivalent cargo

- **Length:** 57 feet 1 inch with rotors

- **Width:** 8 feet 7 inches (fuselage)

- **Height:** 14 feet 5 inches

- **Internal Fuel Capacity:** 209 gallons

- **Empty weight:** 5,215 pounds

- **Gross weight:** 9,040 pounds

- **Max takeoff weight:** 9,500 pounds

- **Powerplant:** Lycoming T53L13 Turbo — Jet engine, 1,400 shaft horsepower

- **Main rotor diameter:** 48 feet

Performance

- **Maximum speed:** 135 mph (217 km/h; 117 kn)

- **Cruise speed:** 125 mph (201 km/h; 109 kn)

- **Range:** 315 miles (274 nmi; 507 km)

- **Maximum endurance:** 2.4 hours

- **Service ceiling:** 19,390 feet, dependent on factors such as weight, air temperature, etc.

- **Rate of climb:** 1,755 feet per minute

Armament 7.62 mm machine guns, 2.75-inch (70 mm) rocket pods

Glossary

Airborne Unit — a paratrooper unit where soldiers used parachutes to jump out of airplanes

AC — Aircraft Commander

Air Mission Commander — The Air Mission Commander commands and controls all aviation elements on a specific mission or operation

AO — Area of operations

Ash & Trash — The term we used to describe administrative flights

AHC — Assault helicopter company

ARC — American Red Cross

Attacks by fire — When the enemy fired weapons at us but did not assault with troops

Bikini — Call sign for the 170th Assault Helicopter Company

Bingo — A phrase used to indicate that an aircraft was overhead

Blue One — The call sign used on the radio by the 1st lift platoon commander

CCC — Command and control central

C & C helicopter — Command and control helicopter

"C" model guns — UH-1C gunships

Carpet bombing — Used to describe the heavy bombing from Air Force B-52 bombers

CA — Combat assault

Covey — Call sign used by the Special Forces SOG team flying in a FAC aircraft

Cowboy — The nick name of a South Vietnamese Air Force helicopter pilot

Daniel Boone — The code name used for SOG operations in Cambodia

Dog Bone — The name given to a 4th Infantry Division Fire Support Base south of Dak To

Donut Dollies — The term used for the Red Cross women serving in Vietnam

Dragon Mountain — The local name used for a large mountain near Camp Holloway in Pleiku Province

Flying tanks — A description used for the A1-E Douglas Skyraider aircraft

FAC - Air Force Forward Air Controller

Fast Movers — This was a term we used to identify jet aircraft that were fighter / bombers in support of our operations

FSB — Fire support base

FOB — Forward operating base

Freedom bird — The term used for the commercial jets that were used to fly soldiers home after their tour in Vietnam

Get-home-itis — A term used to describe the

need for a pilot to fly back to home base often in spite of bad weather

Ghost Rider — The call sign used by members of the 189th Assault Helicopter Company

GCA — Ground Control Approach

Guns — The term used to identify attack helicopters usually UH-1Cs

HOBO — The call sign used by Air Force pilots when flying A1-E aircraft

Hotel 9 — A code word used by Special Forces SOG personal to identify a specific location in Laos

IFR — Instrument flight rules

LZ — Landing zone

LZ Xray — The name of the Landing Zone that was used in 1965 by the 1st Cavalry Division during the battle of the Ia Drang Vallery

MACV-SOG - Military Assistance Command Vietnam — SOG

Mayday — A word used by pilots to indicate they had an emergency and were likely to crash

Mustachio — The nickname of a South Vietnamese Air Force helicopter pilot

Pink Panther — The call sign used by flight crews from the 361st Aerial Weapons Company

Prairie Fire — A code word used by Special Forces SOG personnel to identify operations in Laos

RA — Regular Army

Round eyes — A term used to describe any American woman in Vietnam

Run-on landing — A type of landing where the helicopter is landed similar to a fixed wing airplane without coming to a hover

Salem House - A code word used by Special Forces SOG personnel to identify operations in Cambodia

Sandy - The call sign used by Air Force pilots when flying A1-E aircraft

Shinning Brass - A code word used by Special Forces SOG personnel to identify operations in Laos

Short-timer Calendar — Any calendar used by a soldier to mark off the days remaining on his Vietnam tour

Shrimpboats — The call sign for the 179th Medium Lift CH-47 helicopter company located a Camp Holloway

Slick — A slang term for UH — 1 lift helicopters

Snakes — A slang term for AH-1G attack helicopter gunships

SF — Special Forces

SOG — Studies and observation group

String — A term used for the McGuire Rig extraction system used on SOG missions

TAC-E — Stood for tactical emergency

TOC — Tactical operations center

Tactical Emergency — A term used when the combat situation was extremely bad and help was needed as soon as possible

Task sheet — The administrative form used to assign flight missions

Titty Mountain — The slang term used to describe a large mountain located near Camp Holloway in Pleiku Province

Turtle — A term used for a person scheduled as a replacement

Tri-border Area — The area where the three borders of South Vietnam, Cambodia and Laos intersected

Up-country — An expression used to describe being in the Highlands of South Vietnam

VNAF — Vietnamese Air Force

Walked their rounds — When mortar fire is adjusted by the gunner so that shells advance toward the intended target

CPSIA information can be obtained
at www.ICGtesting.com
Printed in the USA
BVHW07s0151070718
520754BV00002B/7/P